"Well-balanced and highly readable, *The Friends We Keep* has all the virtues of good scholarship while being wonderfully suitable for a wide range of readers. Hobgood-Oster has provided a superb example of how to combine scholarship with faith experience and active citizenship. I heartily recommend it."

—*Paul Waldau, President of the Religion and Animals Institute, Bob Barker Lecturer on Animal Law at Harvard Law School, and author of* The Animal Invitation: Religion, Law, Science, and Ethics in a More-Than-Human World

"I hope this is a book to which many will turn. In such lively and engaging writing, as others before her have done for domestic violence and slavery, Hobgood-Oster shines a light on a hidden ethical issue so that we are forced to wake up to practices that have been tolerated and reinforced by Christians and our theology."

—*Wendy Farley, Professor of Religion, Emory University*

D1113375

The Friends We Keep

Unleashing Christianity's Compassion for Animals

Laura Hobgood-Oster

BAYLOR UNIVERSITY PRESS

Cover Design by Nicole Weaver, Zeal Design Studio
Cover images © iStockphoto.com/Eric Isselée, lillis-
          photography, alaettin yıldırım
Book Design by Diane Smith

Library of Congress Cataloging-in-Publication Data

Hobgood-Oster, Laura, 1964-
   The friends we keep : unleashing Christianity's compassion for animals / Laura Hobgood-Oster.
      p. cm.
   Includes bibliographical references and index.
   ISBN 978-1-60258-264-4 (pbk. : alk. paper)
   1. Animals--Religious aspects--Christianity. 2. Animal welfare--Religious aspects--Christianity. 3. Human-animal relationships--Religious aspects--Christianity. I. Title.
   BT746.H53 2010
   241'.693--dc22
                                        2010019356

Printed in the United States of America on acid-free paper with a minimum of 30% pcw recycled content.

This book is dedicated to my nephews
Waylon Christopher
and
Johnny David
in the hope that the world will still be full of lots
of animals when they both grow up.

Jesus left that place and went away to the district of Tyre and Sidon. Just then a Canaanite woman from that region came out and started shouting, "Have mercy on me, Lord, Son of David; my daughter is tormented by a demon." But he did not answer her at all. And his disciples came and urged him, saying, "Send her away, for she keeps shouting after us." He answered, "I was sent only to the lost sheep of the house of Israel." But she came and knelt before him, saying, "Lord, help me." He answered, "It is not fair to take the children's food and throw it to the dogs." She said, "Yes, Lord, yet even the dogs eat the crumbs that fall from their masters' table." Then Jesus answered her, "Woman, great is your faith! Let it be done for you as you wish." And her daughter was healed instantly.

—*Matthew 15:21-28*[*]

Contents

List of Illustrations

Preface

Writing a History of Animals in Christianity

> *Somewhere every culture has an imaginary zone for what
> it excludes, and it is that zone we must try to remember
> today.*
>
> —*Catherine Clement*[1]

The end of 2009 might someday be known as the time when a new trend started in Christian worship—church services for dogs. Now, certainly dogs had been in church before that in less formal ways. But for the first time they were getting some news coverage. Early in November a reporter from the Associated Press, Gillian Flaccus, contacted me to ask some questions about a story she was writing. Covenant Presbyterian Church in Los Angeles was initiating a new worship service, Canines at Covenant. Miniature dachshunds, pit bulls, dog beds and biscuits, and about thirty humans gathered for this trial run. According to Rev. Tom Eggebeen it was quite a success. The congregation decided to try this for several reasons, including the shifting family structure in the United States and the prevalence of pets as important companions particularly for single or older adults.[2] Dogs have lived with humans for at least fifteen thousand years; we have evolved in many ways together, shaping each others' lives and deaths. Including dogs in our religious lives simply makes sense. Or does it?

Over the course of the last two thousand years, Christianity was born, grew up in the Mediterranean world, became the religion of an empire, then of empires, and transformed itself as it moved around the globe. During that time animals have come and gone in the tradition, usually without much notice. The ox and ass are taken for granted in nativity scenes, the dove descends upon Jesus at his baptism, psalms and hymns praise the glory of God's creation, including all of the animals. Noah's ark is usually one of the first Bible stories that young children learn as images of cuddly animals in pairs peer over the edge of a boat in their bedrooms. Yet even with this dramatic presence, animals are still often noticeably absent. This book is my attempt to find those animal voices in Christianity, voices that I believe strengthen and enrich the tradition immensely.[3]

We humans live with other animals in our midst, yet we forget to notice their presence or even consciously choose to ignore them as we deem them insignificant. Yet deep down I think most of us know that we cannot live without them and we really don't want to. Animals enter our lives every day in various ways—as food, as clothing, as objects of entertainment or sport, as coinhabitants of the earth, and as personal, beloved companions. But we rarely if ever consider the impact of our religious belief systems on animals or the impact of animals on our religions. What, if anything, do animals have to do with, in, and for Christianity? And does Christianity have anything to say about the current state of affairs for animals? For complicated historical reasons, I think animals have been forgotten by Christianity, at least in relationship to the religious tradition itself. While some individual Christians include animals in their circle of compassion, the tradition seems to have collective amnesia about the role of the rest of God's creatures in religion and in life as a whole. Though they are very much present, they have become absent. In the pages that follow I hope to find them again.

The model that I use in much of my writing and research is that used by some of the historians who have worked diligently to find the stories of women in the history of religious traditions. Just as it is difficult to find accounts of animals, the stories of women have been difficult to reconstruct because the dominant texts of most traditions often excluded their perspectives and biographies. One of the best examples of this undertaking is the seminal work *In Memory of Her* written by Elisabeth Schussler Fiorenza. In this book the author struggles with the challenges of recovering the voices of women in Christian history. Seeking to respond to contemporary concerns, notably of the feminist movement of the 1980s, Schussler Fiorenza's project was to examine women's contributions to Christianity throughout its history. As she states in the introduction to the book, the aim was "to interrupt hegemonic historical discourses" and "to bring about change by repudiating the 'commonsense' cultural premise of the historical invisibility of most women and disenfranchised men in dominant historiographies."[4] In other words, Schussler Fiorenza sought to make present voices in the history of Christianity whose absence was simply assumed or whose presence was counted as insignificant. This project required considering different ways of framing history itself and placed history in conversation with contemporary challenges and questions. In so doing, she helped to ignite a wealth of feminist reconstructions of Christian history in the three decades that followed. In this book I humbly aspire to do the same kind of work that Schussler Fiorenza did—recovering lost voices. Here, however, I attempt to do so for other-than-human animals. While their voices might be less literal ones, at least in the common human perception and definition of voices, their lives are still a significant part of the story.

But how does one even begin to consider a history of animals, indeed a history of animals in the context of an apparently completely human endeavor such as religion? History is usually based on the recovery of voices, even those that are hidden between the lines of other voices. Schussler Fiorenza claimed that "current scholarly theory and research are deficient because they neglect women's lives and contributions and construe humanity and human history as male."[5] Still, it is *human* history, ergo there is a voice present, even if it is at the margins or often silenced. Might one also claim that current scholarly theory and research are deficient because they neglect the lives of all of the other animals and construe human history as isolated from the myriad animals who surround us day in and day out? Can Christianity be understood without knowing that bees lived at the monasteries, providing the wax for the candles made by these religious communities for worship? Can Christianity be fully comprehended without knowing the stories of the wild animals who provided food for saints? Indeed, can Christianity be understood without consideration of the sparrows, the fish, and the donkeys with whom Jesus lived, those animals included in his life and in his parables? And, in the contemporary world, can Christianity be a fully engaged, living tradition if it does not consider how the chicken got into the casserole at the potluck supper?

Erica Fudge, a scholar who writes about the history of animals, claims that it is a history of "the most unnoticed of all."[6] She goes on to note that there are obvious problems with writing such a history, particularly since animals leave no documents. In this book I follow her lead and propose that such a poststructuralist and holistic history is required for a consideration of animals in both the past and the present of Christianity. It is not only a history of ideas, of the human representation of animals. Rather it is a way of thinking about and studying animals that requires us as humans to rethink our own position in relationship to others. We must "reassess the place of the human."[7] By placing animals in the history of Christianity, might we not begin to reconfigure humans in the tradition as well?

On its surface, this reconsideration of the place of the human in the Christian tradition could appear somewhat daunting, particularly since the human incarnation of the divine is such a focal point for the faith. But when carefully and thoughtfully examined, this reconsideration has the potential to reveal a powerful and meaningful insight, one that puts God at the center again, with all of the creatures on Earth as part of this magnificent enterprise of life.

A Note on Sources and Method

It is not always easy to reconstruct the histories of those humans or, in this case, those animals who have not been part of the official or dominant stories. If one is searching for documentation on rulers, military leaders, and wealthy people, it certainly requires research, but information can often been found, and it can be documented. Often those people also wrote something themselves, so we have "primary" sources in their own voice. There is a document trail that can be verified according to the standards of Western scholarship. I am trained in this scholarship so include numerous citations throughout this book.

But it is not always as straightforward when one's subject is animals. They require a different look at history. So while a variety of sources are mined for information on animals, some, though not all, of these sources are less traditional than those normally used for scholarship. As the historical theologian Alex García-Rivera made clear in his book about Martín de Porres, a saint whose story will be central in the next chapter, it is not always the "Big Story" told by some scholars, church leaders, and theologians but the "little stories told by specialists and nonspecialists, by assembly line workers and university professors alike" that often bear the most truth for the most people.[8] I follow García-Rivera's lead and look for many "little stories" to find the animals.

But this approach does not exclude the most central big story, the biblical text, which has been used normatively in scholarship on the history of Christianity and in popular religion for almost two millennia. Though the exegesis and analysis of some of these sacred texts might provide a different lens, I will reference the Bible consistently to provide the requisite foundation in the tradition. Along with the biblical text, other early apocryphal and extracanonical texts will also be important to this look at animals.

However, some of the most significant pieces of information about animals can be gleaned from popular religion, these "little stories"—the legends of saints, images in churches, rituals for the masses. Hagiographies, or the edifying stories of saints, provided an introduction into the Christian life for masses of people of faith for centuries. Most villages in Europe had a patron saint whose life and miracles were celebrated on a feast day particular to that community. The stories of the more broadly recognized saints were passed from city to city. Specific incidents in their lives were used to decorate churches, and some of the great works of European art portray saints' activities. People gathered for worship would learn these stories and model their lives after these most holy, canonized friends of God. With amazing frequency, animals accompany these saints. So throughout the book stories of saints provide an important foundation for rethinking our relationships with animals.

Unfortunately, in my opinion, many of these stories are less familiar to the majority of Christians than they were five hundred years ago. For complex historical reasons, one outcome of the Protestant Reformation was ending the veneration of saints. They were seen as too closely connected to particular ritual practices and belief systems of the Roman Catholic Church. I suggest that reconsidering their stories might be worthwhile for all Christians, even those outside of the Catholic and Eastern Orthodox communions. Also, as will become obvious in the pages that follow, for many contemporary Christians in predominantly Catholic countries, particularly in Central and South America, saints are still central to daily life. They are also still commonly recognized throughout Europe. And some Protestant congregations are actually including them again, at least one of them, Saint Francis of Assisi, the patron saint of animals.

It is not always as easy to trace the genealogy of these sources that recount the lives and miracles of saints. For example, legends of saints exist in oral traditions that are recorded as popular literature, appear in the stained glass windows of churches, become part of children's stories, or are reenacted as part of the festival on their feast day. These stories of animals are important to consider. It is from these popular accounts and visual images more than from much of the official literature or the formal theology that the belief systems of the majority of Christians throughout history can be found.

That stated, throughout the text I have made it a point to follow the trail behind the popular stories as exhaustively as possible. If, for example, a saint's legend includes a story about a particular companion animal, I searched to find support for the account in as many different hagiographies or iconographies as possible. If the story is well represented, then we can assume that it is part of the broad popular legend associated with that saint and that many people were aware of the story and used it as a guide in their religious lives.

For more contemporary issues, such as animals in sport or as food, that required gathering timely information, I relied on government sources, industry reports, and recognized, reputable news journals. Once again, I followed through to confirm this information as thoroughly as possible and in all cases note where I located statistics or claims.

This was not an easy book to write. I am trained as a historian of religions, with historical theology (or the interaction between religious beliefs and historical situations) as my primary mode of approaching subjects of research, writing, and teaching. My tendency is to write as if I am addressing an audience who reads this type of literature frequently. But in this case I am also writing about a subject (or, more accurately, subjects) that is much more important to me, animals. And the goal is to open this discussion to as many ears and voices as possible, particularly to those in faith communities who are wondering about animals in Christianity. With that in mind, I attempted to think differently about who I am in this conversation between believers, scholars, people who care about animals, contemporary cultural forces, history, and animals. Hopefully that voice comes through in the words on the pages that follow.

Acknowledgments

Books such as this one are drawn from countless experiences and a wonderful crowd of companions. I want to thank as many of those companions here as I can recall.

First, this book was truly a collaborative effort with my editor, Nicole Smith Murphy. She carefully read draft after draft and made copious, amazingly helpful comments. Without her encouragement and her persistence, I would not have completed this book. Nicole is also a dedicated dog rescue volunteer, so we share a common understanding of the urgency of this issue for people of faith.

I also want to thank the dogs, cats, staff, and volunteers of the Georgetown Animal Shelter and Georgetown Animal Outreach. In particular I want to thank Jackie Carey, the shelter manager. While all of the animals who come into this place cannot be saved, they are all treated with respect and love while they are there.

A number of faculty colleagues at Southwestern University and elsewhere helped me clarify ideas and taught me many things about animals that I did not know. To these colleagues I offer a special thank you: Jimmy Smith, Elaine Craddock, Fay Guarraci, Steven Schapiro, Paul Waldau, Donna Haraway, Marc Bekoff, Carol Adams, Jay McDaniel, Belden Lane, Mary Evelyn Tucker, and John Grim. I also want to thank the students at Southwestern who participated in many discussions in "Going to the Dogs" and "Animals and Religion," my two favorite classes.

In recent years the Humane Society of the United States has also reached out to communities of faith in their quest to extend compassion to as many animals as possible; their efforts are bearing wonderful fruit.

As always, the support of my family is immeasurable—my parents, who taught me to love animals; my sister, brother, and sister-in-law, who continue to offer hospitality to otherwise homeless pets; and my nephews, who inspire me each day. My family is larger than that, though; there are lots of dogs and cats who remind me that our circle of kinship must be expanded: Codi, Cooper, Dozier, Wink, Hummer, Gus, Mathilda, and Princess. I could list hundreds of dogs who fill my life with joy, and with sadness, in the dog rescue world; several are mentioned in the pages that follow.

And my most sincere thanks to my spouse, Jack, who is so very patient and kind with me and with all of the dogs who come and go from our home.

Introduction
Even Dogs Deserve the Crumbs

Are your angels really hovering in the sky?
Because I think I just saw one walking by
Leaving paw prints in the snow
Cloven tracks in the mud
A slug trail on the sidewalk
Hoofprints . . .
How near they are. How holy they are.

—*Carol Adams*[1]

The Georgetown, Texas, city animal shelter probably sees too much of me. While my professional life revolves around a university, its classes and students and intellectual work, my "real" life revolves around dogs and many other animals. For almost a decade the kind and often quite stressed humans who work day in and day out at the city's shelter have allowed me to help find homes for the many dogs who end up there. They get the hard jobs of euthanizing the animals who are in pain, who have behavioral issues that they deem dangerous, or who just happen to land at the shelter when it is too full to take in any additional dogs or cats.[2] Though some stories are heartwrenching for me as well, I usually get more happy stories of dogs landing on sofas in their new homes and cats curling up on their adopter's lap.

Questions from the religious tradition that filled my life as a child of the church, the intellectual practice that draws me into conversations with theories and their applications as a professor, and the activist engagement that takes me into animal shelters and slaughterhouses are the resources that drive me to fill the pages of this book. I am confident, and make this claim without hesitation, that religious traditions and spirituality do have much to offer if humans want to live differently with animals. By the same token, I am confident that thinking about animals and how they are included in our religious beliefs and practices will only enrich our religious traditions and provide compassionate and meaningful outlets for engagement with the world.

Consider the account of Jesus and the Canaanite woman reported in the Gospel of Matthew and quoted in the front matter of this book.[3] It is one of many stories in Scripture that open doors into the world of animals in the Christian tradition. Not only is it loaded with meaning and dripping with various possibilities for interpretation, but it brings *real animals* into the conversation. As many exegetes have detailed, this story certainly has much to say about issues of ethnic identity and the comparative worth of human beings at a particular point in history. It is amazing as well that Jesus is corrected and accepts the challenge presented by this outsider, the Canaanite woman. And, yes, the dogs eating the crumbs are likely used metaphorically by both Jesus and the woman. But might these dirty dogs eating the scraps below the table *also be real animals*? It is based on this possibility that I begin this journey exploring the relationship between humans and other-than-human animals in Christianity. They have been symbols in the form of lambs and doves, they have been accidental onlookers and maybe even unwilling participants; imagine for example the horses ridden to the Crusades or on Methodist circuits on the American frontier. And they have been real bodies present in the midst of Christian practices, beliefs, and rituals in many cultures for two millennia.

As the twenty-first Christian century moves along, the state of animals, both human and other, on the earth is in constant flux with habitats shifting and species disappearing.[4] We humans have shaped the current state of the planet to such an extent that we must recognize our impact and our import and take responsibility for how we act and on whom we act. While issues like climate change and environmental degradation as a whole continue to be somewhat controversial in certain communities, scientific research and direct observation by lay people strongly suggest that humans are changing the face of the planet. In so doing, we are drastically impacting the lives of other humans, of ourselves and our descendants, and of the other animals who live here with us. Christianity is the single largest religious tradition; over two billion practitioners identify with it globally. As humans face different and very complicated challenges, we need to ask: does the Christian tradition have anything to say about how humans live in relationship with other animals? I believe it does. The rich history of Christianity, through its texts, its rituals, its images, and its practices, actually provides copious resources to instruct Christians and provide compassion for animals in today's complicated world.

What issues are the most pressing? Through recent books like Michael Pollan's *The Omnivore's Dilemma* and Barbara

Kingsolver's *Animal, Vegetable, Miracle*, we learn about important issues related to animals in the food production system, and we will consider these huge impacts. In addition to animals in the food production system (an issue we will explore later), issues surrounding animals as companions and pets, animals used in sport or for entertainment, and animals as coinhabitants of this planet or as neighbors in the creation need to be considered. Throughout Christian history each of these issues has been pondered and addressed in numerous ways, albeit sometimes in ways that are hidden or at least not obvious unless one is deliberately paying attention. Drawing on these plentiful resources, however, provides a foundation for contemporary Christian action and theological development.

And the time today is ripe for such discussion. Consider, as one example of this debate in Christianity, the dialogue between a writer at *Christianity Today* and Kay Warren, the wife of well-known pastor Rick Warren of Saddleback Church. In her blog, posted on her.meneutics, Kay Warren wrote that she was "emotionally duped, then angered, by a heart-tugging television ad about suffering animals." Why? She believed that animals are not worthy of such compassion. As she wrote, "Jesus didn't die for animals; he gave his all for human beings."[5] I beg to differ. And so did the author of an opinion piece published in *Christianity Today* who suggested that it is not only appropriate but central to Christianity to acknowledge that "animals have worth and dignity."[6] Based on the early Christian memory of the words of Jesus, I wonder whether Warren's claim is, at the least, a bit too broad and, more likely, quite presumptuous. But I also wonder how many other Christians initially agree with her sentiment, thoughtlessly really, only to rethink their assessment when greeted by their dog after a long day at work or when pondering the world without polar bears or butterflies.

According to Christian tradition and history as it developed over the last two thousand years, Jesus died to save humanity, though some might consider it more important that he lived for humanity. But does that exclude the possibility of his and, by extension, Christianity's compassion for all of the other animals as well? There are numerous stories of Jesus' connections with animals. Animals surround Jesus at his birth, he spends forty days in the wilderness with the wild beasts, he tells parables articulating God's care for the birds of the air, he instructs his followers to break the rules of the Sabbath in order to pull a sheep from a pit. Yes, Jesus also sends demons into a group of swine and drives them off the edge of a cliff. But the stories are full of indications that Jesus paid serious attention to animals other than humans. There is some ambiguity, but it would be a misinterpretation to suggest that wanton cruelty to animals would have been an acceptable behavior in his eyes or that total lack of care for them was a default or even acceptable position.

Along with the ambiguity of some of its sacred texts, the history of Christianity reveals both a vision of compassion for other animals and a justification for the abuse of or at least the disregard for them. Some of the topics might seem, at first glance, to have little to do with Christianity, so throughout, historical connections provide a foundation for a lens through which the contemporary situation is examined. Certainly, for example, animals symbolize particular ideas in the tradition. But I contend that they are also *real* animals, and it is from that point that this work begins—considering real animals as part of the circle of Christian concern. Thinking about animals as only and always mere symbols is a way of escaping our responsibility to real animals. It serves to reinforce human superiority and dominance over compassion and connection.[7] We all exist in webs of relationships

that cannot be denied; to do so would be a delusion at best
and hubris at worst. Religious traditions rely on animals to
help establish patterns of existence, sets of rituals, and com-
plexes of relationships with others, both divine others and
fully earthly others.

Yet in the last several hundred years Christianity has been
hesitant, at times, to include animals in either its ethical or
its theological systems. Without addressing the issue of "the
animal," Christianity not only lives in a potentially dangerous bubble, but it risks becoming increasingly narcissistic and
marginal to the world as we know it, and as we are making it. Thus, this book is both a religious-environmental history and a contemporary theology. It is grounded in the idea
that humans must recognize the risks of anthropocentrism,
of thinking that and acting as if humans are the center of all
that is. When anthropocentrism is wedded to religious ideas,
it becomes a major factor in both environmental destruction
and the rapid march toward massive species extinction that
humans instigated in the last several centuries. But this book
is also written in the firm belief that all religions, in this case
Christianity, can provide powerful resources that will coun-
ter destructive anthropocentrism and, hopefully, call humans
into a new relationship with our fellow Earth inhabitants.

Years ago I traveled to Italy for a conference on sustain-
ability in the liberal arts. Two undergraduate students went
with me, and I asked them to look for animals in the churches.
Their initial response was one of confusion and skepticism;
actually they thought I was either living in a fairy tale or teas-
ing them. These students were sure that they would not find
any animals in the churches. However, several days later they
returned with eyes bulging. Animals were everywhere in the
artwork and the stories of these medieval monuments to God
and to faith. Dogs appear in images of the Last Supper, ravens

Saint Anthony Abbot, the patron saint of animals,
as he is often pictured, with a pig.
Statue at the Church of Saint Eusebius in Rome.
Photo by author.

are shown whispering in the ears of saints, bees adorn the tops of pillars, a big ox kneels before the relics of a saint, and real pigeons ask for bread in the piazzas in front of the churches.

As will hopefully become evident in the chapters that follow, animals have been subjects, participants, and companions in the history of Christianity. The canonical Scriptures (the Bible), the extracanonical early texts (apocryphal gospels, stories of martyrs), the lives of saints in the Middle Ages (hagiographies), and the ritual lives of normal people throughout Christianity's history all include animals. And this is just to name a few places where they are found. Historically the majority of humans have lived in the company of myriad other animals. It is an anomaly in human history to be as removed from other animals as most urban and suburban people in the U.S. are today. Sadly, the primary encounter we have with other animals is when they are already processed for eating, placed on the grocery store shelves. The living animals we do encounter are sometimes pets (increasingly important figures on many levels) or are framed as exotic wild species, often only seen in documentaries or on Animal Planet. Many human lives are empty of animals, and we find ourselves in a lonely situation.

Yet when we humans open our eyes and look holistically at our stories and our lives, we cannot help but realize that we are not who we are without other animals surrounding us. But we do have the power to make them invisible, or at least we think we do. And too often we act as if they do not matter. It is both this power to render animals invisible and this potential for compassion that we need to take very seriously.

Through the pages of this book I will try to make present the animals in the history of Christianity and then to make connections between the history and the contemporary world. We will see and experience them as Christians have for generations—as companions, as unfortunate prisoners in the arenas of Rome, as recipients and givers of hospitality, and as food. With these stories of our shared history in mind, each chapter turns to contemporary issues and asks how Christians might reconsider animals in light of this shared history. Finally, then, we can pose this question: might Christianity also be "good news for animals?"[8]

Chapter 1

What a Friend We Have
Our Animal Companions

For many of us, love for creation deepens through the relationship we form with our pets, particularly our dogs. By their very nature and need, dogs draw us out of ourselves: they root us in nature, making us more conscious of the mystery of God inherent in all things.

—*The Monks of New Skete*[1]

Jazz was scared to death. Who wouldn't be? She and her two puppies had just weathered Hurricane Katrina in New Orleans and now, several days later, they were in an animal control facility in Houston. The first time I saw her, Jazz was being wheeled on a cart in a crate with two little puppies underneath her, hunkered down, shaking. Of course, Jazz did not have a name at that point; her name came later, along with Gumbo and Chickory for the two six-week-old puppies. They came into my little rescue group, Georgetown Animal Outreach, with a number of other desperate dogs and cats from New Orleans: Mardi Gras, Rouge, Jax, Nola, Mississippi Queen, and so on.[2]

Jazz, a Hurricane Katrina rescue dog. Photo by author.

Houston, Texas, about two hours east of where I live, was flooded with refugees from the hurricane, both human and animal. The pounds and shelters were overflowing with dogs and cats who were left homeless in New Orleans after the storm or had already landed in shelters before the storm hit. We, fortunately, were in a position to help; Georgetown, the small city north of Austin where I live and teach, had just built a new animal shelter. Most of the old one was still standing, and the city agreed that our small group of volunteers could use it to house Jazz, Chickory, Gumbo, and their companions. In two big vans, with lots of dog crates and cat carriers, our little crew headed to Houston to help with the influx of animals.

All the dogs I encounter while volunteering in dog rescue are special, but from the moment our eyes met, I knew that Jazz was going to be one of those who stole my heart completely. She was a petite dog, a black-and-white basenji-terrier-looking girl. Still nursing her two puppies, Jazz was worn-out, with a rough coat and tired eyes. I suspect she was a homeless dog in New Orleans; at her first trip to the veterinarian, we found out she had heartworms, hookworms, and whipworms. She needed some time to heal.

Two months later, after her puppies had already been adopted and she had been vaccinated and spayed, we were still treating Jazz for her various ailments. But it was time to move her into a foster home and out of the old shelter that we were shutting down. I loaded her up into my car and headed for the foster home with one of my responsible and caring college students. Ten minutes after transferring Jazz to her foster's car, my cell phone rang, connecting me to a frantic voice on the other end telling me that Jazz had bolted terrified from the car and was running loose and scared on campus. By the time I got there, a group of students had corralled her into the tennis courts, so at least she was safe from the busy streets. But they could not get her to come close to them. She was practiced in the skills of darting away from humans (Jazz had probably escaped the dog catchers in New Orleans for years). I walked through the gate and called her name. She bolted toward me and jumped into my arms, then buried her face under my neck with a sigh of relief as if to say, "Thank you, I thought I was alone again, but you came back."[3]

Well, not just any home would do for Jazz. We are always as careful as possible placing dogs in permanent homes, but I was determined that Jazz would go to someone who would keep me posted on her for the rest of her life, someone I trusted completely. A childhood friend of mine, who is now a minister in Michigan, eventually adopted Jazz and gave her a loving home. Jazz goes to church with Linda or Chris (he is a minister as well, at another church) and sleeps on the sofa or curled up in bed by them. Jazz has a birthday party every year, and Linda always keeps me up-to-date on how Jazz is doing. I even get to see her occasionally. Jazz is a blessing in their lives, as much as she continues to be one in mine.

As we start our investigation into animals and Christianity, pondering animals as companions seems like a good place to start. These are our most personal and direct relationships, where we live with and care about real, living creatures on an individual basis. Contemplating their lives and their history in Christianity provides a firm foundation for thinking about all animals differently.

Consider this quotation from Tobit, a book in the Apocrypha: "The young man went out and the angel went with him; and the dog came out with him and went along with them" (6:1-2). In this quotation, the Scripture writer conveys that it is just assumed that the dog will be there, go along with the man and the angel, Tobias and Raphael. In much of the religious artwork depicting these characters from the book of Tobit, the dog is portrayed playing at their feet, helping them to catch fish, or watching the angel fly back to heaven.[4]

Just as Tobias in the book of Tobit went out with his dog on an important journey, so too do we navigate our world with companion animals in our midst. Even if one does not live with a cat on their sofa or a dog begging under the table or a hamster spinning on a wheel, companion animals are central to the lives of increasing numbers of humans globally and, to a certain extent and in varying ways, have been for millennia.

This chapter cannot begin to address companion animals as a whole, which is actually a huge category. Think about it. We humans are in relationship with microscopic species, with beetles, spiders, bees and ants, and countless other living beings. There are many of these without whom we simply would not be here. While it would be worthwhile to write about these vital and life-sustaining connections (as a matter of fact, I think it is urgent to consider these smallest of beings in the context of Christianity), there is not enough space here to address these complicated interactions that sustain our lives in countless ways. Still, I hope that considering those most noticeable, the ones we sometimes call our pets, will shed light on all of our connections, including those with the tiniest of animals.

Why Animal Companions Matter

Amy and Karma inspire me whenever I see them. They focus on each other, work for each other, take care of each other, and go just about everywhere together. When I met Amy she was a first-year student at the college where I teach, and Karma had not yet entered her life. Amy was born with cerebral palsy and needed to use a wheelchair to maneuver the campus. An eager, bright student, Amy chose to be a religion major, which made me quite glad.

As is the case for many dogs, Karma, a beautiful yellow Labrador retriever, had a tough start followed by a really rough patch. She obviously had not been in the best of homes, so Karma ended up in a municipal animal shelter and was heartworm positive (sound familiar?), which is often, as mentioned above, a death sentence for dogs who end up in shelters. But Texas Hearing and Service Dogs (THSD), an organization that pulls dogs from shelters if they have the right "drive" to be a service dog, tested Karma, took her from the shelter, and, in dog rescue lingo, "saved" her (language that is a bit presumptuous on our part, but those of us who do dog rescue use that term all the time). THSD treated her heartworms; gave her a caring, loving foster home; and got her back into good health, all the while working with her to craft the skills she would need to be a helping dog. Karma was on the road to a whole new life.

Fortunately, as fate would have it, a volunteer with THSD knew both Amy and Karma and quickly decided they would be a perfect match. And they were. Both gave each other new freedom, new opportunities, new possibilities, and a whole new way of being. Karma works hard picking things up off the floor for Amy, opening doors if needed, and doing any number of other tasks that are difficult for Amy with her disability. But there is also an intangible something they do for each other. I'm not sure that words can capture their connection. But Karma looks at Amy with a kind of adoration that speaks more loudly than any words ever could. Amy and Karma's human-dog partnership is amazing and inspiring to witness.[5]

As you have now more than realized, I have a deep fondness for dogs; and in that vein, for almost ten years I have team taught a course to introduce first-year undergraduate students to critical thinking and writing skills called "Going to the Dogs." An outstanding colleague in kinesiology, Dr. Jimmy Smith, and I spend nine weeks introducing new college students to various ideas about the history of dogs; their physiology, culture, and impact on humans; and, finally, the state of dogs in the twenty-first century. While these students have often been around dogs for most of their lives, few have ever really *thought* deliberately or specifically about them before. Most are amazed to learn how long we humans have made dogs a part of our lives. According to even the most conservative estimates, humans and dogs have lived together for at least fifteen to twenty thousand years. Some researchers believe this relationship has existed even longer—for fifty or even one hundred thousand years.[6] Whatever the length of time, however, after reading and studying and observing, I am certain: humans would not be who we are without dogs and dogs would not be who they are without humans. Together we are truly companion species.

But what does this human-dog relationship have to do with the history of Christianity? Indeed, what do our relationships with companion animals in general have to do with this religious tradition? As we will see later, an investigation into the history and theology of Christianity reveals overwhelming praise for companion species and companion animals. But first a definition is in order. What are "companion animals" anyway? How did dogs become dogs? How did cats become cats? After one learns this amazing history, the stories of deep connections between humans and pets make more sense. Scenes of people refusing to leave their pets behind even in the midst of a tragic flood and hurricane become even more understandable.

A Brief History of Humans and Our Pets

In her intriguing work *The Companion Species Manifesto*, Donna Haraway, a biologist and philosopher of science and technology, offers a helpful insight that is focused on dogs but can be expanded to most companion animals: "There cannot be just one companion species; there have to be at least two to make one. It is in the syntax; it is in the flesh. Dogs are about the inescapable, contradictory story of relationships—co-constitutive relationships in which none of the partners pre-exist the relating, and the relating is never done once and for all."[7] In other words, humans are in ongoing relationships with other species, and those relationships shape both us and them. In the case of certain animal species, the ones that I will be addressing here, humans are being formed by this constant companionship. Which animals comprise these positions of "companion" might change throughout history or from one geographic area to another. So, for example, camels are companion species in some dry, desert climates, while Siberian huskies are companion species in arctic climates. But humans have lived with domesticated animals as companion species for thousands of years, though just a very few of these animals ended up as pets. The process of actually merging other animals into human life to create what we call domesticated animals is a long and slow one.[8] What does domestication entail?

Through an obviously complex process, as certain animals who live in a close relationship with humans adapt to this new ecological niche, they undergo changes in diet, behavior, physical composition, and reproductive processes that differentiate them from their counterparts in the wild.[9] While it has sometimes been assumed that this process resulted from human intention, in other words, that a human saw a wild boar and decided to create a pig, recent theories suggest that the various processes at different times and places over the last twenty millennia were much more organic. The transformation from the wolf (*canis lupus*) to the dog (*canis familiaris*) is the most striking tale.

According to physiologist and geographer Jared Diamond, there are six requisite criteria for animal species to become domesticated: flexible diet, fast maturity rate, ability to breed in captivity, nonaggressive disposition, tolerance of threat (so they do not run away from humans), and "follow the leader dominance hierarchies" (so humans can be the "pack leader").[10] With this general rubric in mind, one can picture the process of moving from "wild" to "domesticated" for any number of species. Dogs were likely the first domesticated animal, living, as I mentioned earlier, with humans since at least 15,000 years ago. Dogs actually probably assisted in the domestication process of the later animals, by helping to gather the wild predecessors of the sheep and goats, for example.

Pets, and certainly dogs, are a small category compared to the myriad domesticated animals who have impacted human life over the millennia and into the twenty-first century. And the line between working companion animal and pet has been somewhat blurry. But in general pets are not required to work or function in a way that is economically beneficial, though they might still be emotionally beneficial and might still perform certain helpful tasks such as alerting humans to an imminent danger. Just as other domesticated animals vary from place to place and from time to time, so do the animals who become "pets."

While it is likely that humans have informally kept certain selected animals as pets in some manner for thousands of years, most of the earliest evidence of petkeeping is connected to the wealthy and to nobility. This makes sense for a couple of reasons. First, it is very hard to find any evidence of economically disadvantaged classes having pets, because we have very few records about the everyday lives of the masses of people in history. Second, in order to have pets, humans need to have sufficient resources to feed an excess animal— one who is not working or providing food. But we do know that the wealthy did have pets, even in the far distant past. For example, the Pekingese dog was originally bred in China over two thousand years ago, and ownership was restricted to royalty. Stories of their origin are steeped in Chinese Buddhist legend. Historically, it seems that these dogs were servants at the imperial court and would even carry the robes of the royalty in the palace.[11] The Maltese, a small dog from the

Mediterranean though possibly with Asian roots, is another breed with connections to ancient petkeeping. Images of this dog appear on Egyptian and Greek art that is well over two thousand years old. Eventually the Maltese dog traveled to the courts of England and became a favorite of British royalty, including Queen Elizabeth I.

Dogs are the most high-profile pets in many cultures around the world. Their long and complicated connection to humans is probably the reason why this companion animal occupies the courts of the wealthy, appears in the legends of holy people, and fills the hearts of countless ordinary humans. As humans started to establish permanent (or at least semi-permanent) settlements, we created trash piles. Wolves had probably hunted alongside us for generations by that point. Some of those wolves, the ones least likely to be alpha and least likely to flee from humans, began to eat from these trash piles. Over the course of a relatively short period of time, they morphed slightly, then they morphed a little more. Hormonal changes eventually led to characteristics that distinguish the domesticated animals we know today: floppy ears, piebald (white with spots of some color) coats, shortened muzzles, curly tails, and condensed reproductive cycles. Dogs became dogs just as humans became modern humans, and we did so together. Over the course of the next fourteen millennia, humans became directly involved in selecting dogs for particular abilities along with the accompanying physical traits. Thousands of years after the wolf ate from the human trash heap and started on the path to becoming a dog, human intervention led to amazing diversity; dogs are now the most varied species in the world in terms of size.

As we shaped them, they shaped our culture, and the two species emerged together from being hunters and gatherers to being farmers and shepherds. Dogs helped to transport us into arctic climates and hunted us through snowy winters. They gathered sheep from rocky landscapes and killed rats in our expanding, crowded cities. Eventually they became pets for increasing numbers of people, across all socioeconomic classes. In the eighteenth and nineteenth centuries in Europe and America, as other technologies replaced much of the work of dogs, they became status symbols and filled the households of the growing middle class. By 2006 there were over seventy-two million pet dogs in the United States alone.[12]

While cats are a more problematic species when considering the traits of domestication (probably not a surprise for many humans who live with felines), they likely followed the same general path as dogs in adapting to human society, eating from our waste piles and being welcomed as agents of pest control. At the earliest points of interaction with humans, cats were likely "commensal domesticates," animals who lived close to humans but were not necessarily domesticated. We see them too throughout ancient history. Remains of cats were buried with humans on Cyprus, an island to which they are not indigenous, at least nine thousand years ago.[13] Perhaps they came on boats as stowaways. Or perhaps people deliberately imported them.

In ancient Egypt numerous images of the cat-headed goddess Bastet provide evidence of her widespread veneration, thus it is likely that cats were already wandering the streets of Egypt as useful human companions. Cats, it seems, were extremely popular and important members of Egyptian society and were even given elaborate burials at the time of their deaths. As Annemarie Schimmel, a professor of Islam, wisely remarked, "who else would have been able to kill, or at least to scare away, the mice that threatened the greatest wealth of ancient Egypt, the grain stored in the granaries?"[14] Why is Egypt so important in the history of cats? Domesticated cats throughout the world, including eventually all the continents, descended from the domesticated cats of North Africa.[15]

The kind of devotion to cats seen in Egypt spread throughout the Mediterranean world. By the time Islam spread out of Arabia in the seventh and eighth centuries C.E., stories of cats and the prophet Muhammad were gaining popularity. According to folk stories, "the Prophet Muhammad cut off his coat sleeve because he had to get up for prayer and was loath to disturb his cat Muizza," and when a cat "gave birth to her kittens on the prophet's coat . . . he took care of the offspring."[16] Unlike dogs, who are usually considered to be unclean in Muslim cultures, cats are welcome and considered clean.

In the European Middle Ages the story was quite different for cats, however. Pope Gregory IX (1145–1241) associated cats with a sect in southern France that the church deemed evil.[17] In the papal bull *Vox in Rama*, Gregory IX describes what he calls one of their heretical, even evil, rituals:

> At this time a black cat (*gattus niger*), the size of a small dog, with an upright tail descends backwards down a status which is usually at the meeting. The postulant first kisses the cat's rear . . . Then, each member takes his place and after singing some songs, they face the cat in turn. The master says, "Save us" to the cat, and the one next to him states this. Then those present respond three times and say, "We know the master," and four times they say, "and we ought to obey you."[18]

This is the first documented evidence of the cat being demonized, and sadly black cats in particular. Pope Gregory IX's pronouncement began a series of mass slaughters of cats throughout Europe, sometimes designated the Great Cat Massacre. And by the fifteenth century the population of cats in Europe was severely depleted.

Eventually black cats and black dogs were also connected with people, most often women, condemned of witchcraft.[19] In the early fourteenth century in Ireland, for example, Alice Kyteler was charged with having a "familiar" who would "appear to her nightly in various forms including a cat and a shaggy black dog."[20] Condemned to be burned alive, Alice luckily escaped. Stories such as this one abound. Together, numerous women and their pets were executed. Even religious artworks from the European Middle Ages depicted cats as the lurking evil.[21]

However, when the Black (bubonic) Plague began to hit Europe with a vengeance in the middle of the fourteenth century (1348–1350), the value of cats might have been rediscovered. Historians of medicine suggest that the elimination of cats was one cause that helped to strengthen the epidemic as the plague spread rapidly. Later, the reintroduction of cats might have assisted in ending this recurring disease.[22] People in rural areas had kept cats to protect their grain stores from rodents, so these rural cats repopulated much of Europe. Eventually, though cats were both maligned and beloved, they did survive in Europe, moved to the Americas, and became pets. In the early twenty-first century there are over eighty-two million cats in human homes in the United States and many more living in feral colonies.[23] They still serve the purpose of controlling rodent populations throughout the world.

In addition to cats and dogs, a variety of birds have also been kept as pets for centuries. Pigeons and some falcons were kept both as pets and as workers, particularly as carriers of communication in times of war. Some historians suggest that Alexander the Great introduced parrots as pets to the ancient Mediterranean world after observing birds being kept as pets in India; other historians cite evidence of birds in Egyptian hieroglyphics as even earlier signs that point to birds kept in captivity as companions. One definite piece of evidence comes from the Roman poet Ovid (43 B.C.E.–18 C.E.), who wrote of the death of his mistress' pet parrot.[24] Parrots in captivity can live for decades, some for more than forty years. Might the bird (maybe a dove or a pigeon) whom Noah released from the ark to find land be a precursor to these birds?

These short histories of the dog, the cat, and the bird convey a sense of the long, complex relationship humans have with companion animals who are "pets." It is a complicated category, and some animals move in and out of it, poised between the wild and the domesticated, the worker and the pet. Take horses as an example. They still work pulling carriages or entertain as racing thoroughbreds, but they are also beloved pets, therapy animals, and lifelong companions. Reptiles, numerous fish, pigs, ferrets, guinea pigs, and rabbits also find themselves as pets, and the list goes on and on. With just a few prime examples in the forefront—cats, dogs, birds—but with all of these pets in mind, let us turn to the biblical texts and to other sources in the tradition to determine what we can learn about pets from the history of Christianity.

Where Are Pets in the History of Christianity?

And at his gate lay a poor man named Lazarus, covered
with sores, who longed to satisfy his hunger with what fell
from the rich man's table; even the dogs would come and
lick his sores.

—Luke 16:20-21

After reading this excerpt from Jesus' parable about the rich man and Lazarus, one has to ask: Are pets mentioned in the Bible? Well, the answer depends on how one defines "pet." Absolutely, a number of animals that we categorize as pets are mentioned in various biblical texts. For example, recall the dog who was a companion to Tobias and the angel Raphael in the apocryphal book of Tobit. In other passages, such as several mentioned later from Genesis, camels come to wells with people for water. Donkeys see angels and speak. And, as you may recall, in addition to the dogs who attended to Lazarus in the passage from Luke, dogs also attend to Job. And in Genesis, two (or even seven) animals of every kind, presumably pets included, board the ark with Noah. Yet, as we discussed above, pets are a relatively recent phenomenon for most people. It would be a misreading of history to assume that people in the Mediterranean world two thousand years ago understood these animals the same way. Or, then again, would it? Was there a sense of animals as "pets" in the ancient Mediterranean world and in the cultures that produced the Jewish and Christian Scriptures? I admit, evidence is scarce. However, in some of the stories, as a general attitude of care for the animals is made clearly apparent, it does appear that the idea of companion animals as pets was present.

As a prime example, consider the story found in 2 Samuel 12 in which the prophet Nathan is addressing King David:

> "There were two men in a certain city, the one rich and the other poor. The rich man had very many flocks and herds; but the poor man had nothing but one little ewe lamb, which he had bought. He brought it up, and it grew up with him and with his children; it used to eat of his meager fare, and drink from his cup, and lie in his bosom, and it was like a daughter to him. Now there came a traveler to the rich man, and he was loath to take one of his own flock or herd to prepare for the wayfarer who had come to him, but he took the poor man's lamb, and prepared that for the guest who had come to him." Then David's anger was greatly kindled against the man. He said to Nathan,

"As the Lord lives, the man who has done this deserves to
die; he shall restore the lamb fourfold, because he did this
thing, and because he had no pity." (12:1-6)

In telling this story, Nathan was drawing a parallel between
the lamb and Bathsheba, a woman whom King David had
taken from her husband. This raises a complicated issue in
and of itself, since it suggests that Bathsheba, the woman,
is like a pet. But it makes this much clear: connecting to
a beloved animal as a member of the household was not a
foreign concept in this time. David understood this kind of
connection, since he became angry, even to the point of saying the man should die because he killed the pet lamb. And
Nathan obviously found it natural to describe a situation
where a lamb was living inside the house, drinking from the
human's cup and being cared for "like a daughter." All of
which attests to the idea of petkeeping being well-known in
the biblical world.

In addition to the mention of dogs and the poor man's
lamb in the biblical texts, stories of companion animals
abound in the hagiographies of saints. As mentioned in the
preface, these potent, beloved figures in the history of Christianity have influenced the lives of countless Christians who
sought to model their own behavior on that of these martyrs, anchorites, virgins, and hermits. And, according to their
well-known legends, many of these holy men and women
lived with companion animals. Some of these companion
animals are different creatures than those commonly cate-
gorized as pets in contemporary cultures, but it is obvious
from the stories that their relationships were similarly direct,
caring, and personal.

Many of the earliest stories of saints and animals come
from the Celtic Christian areas of Europe—Western France,
Ireland, Scotland, and Wales. Saint Kentigern, the patron

saint of Glasgow, was raised by the holy hermit, Servan, in northern Scotland. Servan loved animals, and one of his dear companions was a robin who "would eat from [his] hand and was wont to perch on his shoulder." Servan told Kentigern and the other boys in his care about the traditional legend of the robin: that this bird bears the stain of sacred blood on its chest because it tried to stop the blood flow from the wound on Jesus' side while he hung on the cross. One day Servan's robin friend was injured (though the legends do not agree on how it happened) and, sadly, the bird died. Kentigern found the robin with his "little head hanging limp, the bright eyes closed, the pretty red breast all dusty and bedraggled." He held the bird in his hand and, making the sign of the cross over the bird, prayed that God might restore life to this small creature. Soon "the small wings quivered and the eyes opened."[25] This tiny companion animal, a beloved pet for the holy hermit, was worthy of the healing power of God.

Numerous other Celtic Christian saints counted animals among their most beloved companions. Saint Kieran, one of the group of early Irish monastic saints known as the Twelve Apostles of Ireland, chose to live a solitary life in order to focus on prayer. As was the case with many saints who lived in the wilderness, animals gathered around them, and as the legends tell, "his principal attendant was a boar."[26] Even the most famous Irish saint, Saint Patrick, had beloved companions. As his hagiographies tell, "every dog reminded him of those dear faithful companions who, during the six years of his slavery, had helped him to guard his master's flocks."[27] Stories of Saint Brigit, one of the patron saints of Ireland, are filled with accounts of animals. Several of these are recounted later in the book and, as you shall see, her love of animals was central to these well-known tales told throughout Celtic Christian communities.[28]

Important stories of companion animals are also found in the hagiographies of southern European saints. In his paintings and iconography, Saint Roch, who lived from 1295 to 1327 in France and Italy, looks like a humble man with his iconic walking stick in hand. He is often easy to identify as Roch, since in his imagery he is usually accompanied by his faithful companion—a dog with a loaf of bread in his mouth. As his legend goes, Roch was born into a wealthy family in southern France late in the thirteenth century. But he had always been a particularly devout person, and he decided to give away everything he owned to become a wandering pilgrim. On his way to Rome, Roch came upon village after village struck by the plague. He worked tirelessly tending to the sick until he finally fell ill with the plague himself. In order not to infect others, the saint headed into the forest and isolation. Miraculously he survived because a dog brought him bread each day and licked his sores to heal them. In the most popular legends of Saint Roch, the two stay together for the remainder of their lives as fellow travelers and, eventually, prisoners together in a jail in northern Italy. They died there, imprisoned with each other. Statues of the saint with his dog companion adorn numerous sanctuaries throughout Europe. Roch is remembered not only as a healer but as a patron saint for dogs. Each year in Bolivia, for example, Saint Roch's feast day (August 16) is counted as the birthday or day of blessing for all dog companions.

Saint Martín de Porres hails from a slightly later period and another continent. He was born in 1579 in Peru to a Spanish father and a freed slave mother from Panama. As a mulatto growing up in the extremely hierarchical culture of sixteenth-century Lima, the "illegitimate" Martín did not have an easy life. By the time he was sixteen, he became a lay worker at the Convento del Santo Rosario, a Dominican community. The work he did in exchange for food and lodging was menial, lowly, and boring. But finally, even though "Indians, blacks and their descendants" were not allowed to be accepted as brothers, Martín became a lay brother at the age of twenty-four.[29] From this point in his life, we begin to hear stories of Martín's compassion for animals. According to Fray Fernando Aragones, a contemporary of Martín's who recorded the saint's deeds, he would distribute food to the poor each day, but before doing so would "give a blessing saying, 'May God increase it through his infinite mercy.'" And, according to Aragones, it seems that that is what happened, "God increased the food through St. Martín's hand, for all ate . . . and all were contented, even the dogs and the cats."[30] Saint Martín also established an animal shelter at his sister's home. There he kept the once stray and sometimes abused dogs and cats that he encountered in Lima.[31]

One of the most popular stories about Saint Martín, however, was recounted by another Dominican brother who one day observed him in the kitchen of the monastery:

> At the feet of St. Martín were a dog and a cat eating peacefully from the same bowl of soup. The friar was about to call the rest of the monks in to witness this marvelous sight when a mouse stuck his head out from a little hole in the wall. St. Martín without hesitation addressed the mouse as if he were an old friend. "Don't be afraid, little one. If you're hungry come and eat with the others." The little mouse hesitated but then scampered to the bowl of soup. The friar could not speak. At the feet of the servant St. Martín, a dog, a cat, and a mouse were eating from the same bowl of soup.[32]

For obvious reasons, Saint Martín eventually, and quite fittingly, became known as the "Saint Francis of the Americas." In his iconography he is pictured standing in an open doorway, a broom in his hand, cats, dogs, and mice gathered peacefully at his feet.

There are numerous other stories of saints and their companion animals. Saint Jerome had a close relationship with a lion; I will tell more about that story in chapter 4. Saint Gertrude of Nivelles, a seventh-century abbess from Belgium, is usually pictured with mice at her feet and is the patron saint of cats. Saint Hilda, an important figure in the history of Christianity in England, befriended snakes and is one of the few figures in Christian history who actually liked these often demonized animals. Saint Agatha is sometimes known as Santo Gato or Saint Cat.[33] And there are many, many more. Thus, both in a few biblical texts and in these hagiographies, the Christian tradition holds strong images and stories of animals as beloved companions. However, in the official doctrines of the church, as evidenced by the papal bull condemning cats, animal companions, sadly, have not usually fared as well.

There is, however, at least one other major figure in Christian history who found inspiration in his dog: Martin Luther, the instigator of the Protestant Reformation and founder of one of the largest Protestant denominations today. Luther's "puppy" Tolpel is mentioned several times in *Table Talk*, the collection of conversations recorded by various guests who dined with Luther. One evening when Tolpel was begging at the table, Luther said with admiration, "Oh, if I could only pray the way this dog watches the meat! All his thoughts are concentrated on the piece of meat. Otherwise he has no thought, wish or hope."[34] At another point when Luther was playing with his Tolpel, he commented that the "dog is a very faithful animal and is held in his esteem if he isn't too ordinary."[35] In early sixteenth-century Germany it seems there were pets, and dogs were begging for the crumbs under Luther's table.

In the last several decades, the importance of companion animals to humans has only grown. It is my hope that stories of some of these saints and their animal friends, as well as these biblical texts, might also assume greater prominence in the tradition's teachings today.

Companion Animals and God

*Faith is never so complete that it is not accompanied by
self-defensiveness. But this is its requirement: that all
beings, not only our friends but also our enemies, not
only man but also animals and the inanimate, be met with
reverence, for all are friends in the friendship of the one to
whom we are reconciled in faith.*

—*H. Richard Niebuhr*[36]

In addition to the stories and biblical texts, we should also consider Christianity's theological foundations. I want to consider a more expansive theological sense of relationship and companionship than has usually been the norm in Christian theology. Based on the stories told above, we can conclude that other animals have been included in circles of care and friendship throughout the history of Christianity. Theology needs to make room for these animals as well. Several theologians and philosophers help lay the foundation for this expanded notion of companionship.

The twentieth-century Jewish philosopher Martin Buber, who influenced numerous Christian theologians, wrote a now-classic text titled *I and Thou*. In this piece Buber presented this idea about the nature of God: "In the beginning is relationship." To Buber, companionship is inherent in God.[37] I know this might sound like an odd or an obvious statement, but evidence in the history, practices, texts, and theological traditions of Christianity reveals this: God likes company. In the quotation that opens this section, H. Richard Niebuhr, one of the most prominent twentieth-century Christian theologians and ethicists, argues that God is in a relationship of friendship with all animals as well as humans and inanimate objects. According to Niebuhr, with God "all are friends."

A wonderful example of this expanded notion of companionship is evident in the lifestyle developed by the Monks and Nuns of New Skete. They make up a vibrant monastic community in the Eastern Orthodox tradition. One of the unique things about this group is that for over thirty years they have lived and worked intentionally with dogs, very much emphasizing the sacred aspect of relationships with dogs and seeing it as central to their spiritual life. They introduce one of their books, *I & Dog* (a very deliberate reflection on Martin Buber's book quoted above), with this statement:

> [Martin] Buber's central intuition is that how we are in relationship with everything in our lives affects our experience of the sacred, and that we realize this effect in the very act of relationship, if only we are open. We humans can and do form mutually inspiring and beneficial relationships with our dog companions, and this experience colors every aspect of our life . . . The tradition in which we stand believes that we already exist in a profound communion with all that is . . . Our dog friends, like life itself, are trying to get our attention. Maybe our canine connection is the missing link, a crucial invitation to respond to this great call to a richer, more abundant banquet of life that is already prepared and waiting.[38]

In other words, the Monks and Nuns of New Skete believe that companion animals invite us to extend outside of ourselves, to come into relationship with the world, with all of God's creation.

Think of the whole story of Genesis in broad strokes. God creates and then continues to nurture the earth and all of the animals who live on it, all, it seems, with the idea of companionship in mind. With each step, God declares "it is good." In Genesis 2, God seeks to find an appropriate partner for the "human" (usually translated as Adam). As you may recall, that quest proves to be a long process and involves lots of animals. One could argue that the end of the process suggests that only another human is an appropriate partner; and that is so—at least, it seems, for purposes of reproduction. But in the meantime, Adam gives names to and gets to know numerous other animals who lived within the garden. The quest for God and then God's quest for the human and for the other animals is to be in relationship.

Why is it that the orthodox telling of the creation stories concludes with the idea that humans are the only fit companions for each other? And, by theological extension, the only fit companions for God? Why is it that the traditional tellings also suggest that God is above and beyond any friendships or relationships? That the entire creation is beholden to God's whim and will? Those assumptions need, I think, to be pressed and questioned—particularly with contemporary understandings of evolution and the origins of the universe in mind. If God is the grounding for and Creator of life, and life, as we know from theories of evolution, is consistently changing, always recreating and evolving, would it not make sense that God is able to be in, and desires to be in, relationships that are fluid, alive, and mutual?

First, throughout the Scriptures God continues to muddle through a variety of, arguably sometimes failed, relationships. In the Hebrew Bible (the Christian Old Testament) the focus is the difficult and ever-evolving relationship between God and the people of Israel. Individuals such as David, Ruth, Abraham, and Jonah provide rich examples of the difficulties of living together as companion species. But God does not limit God's relationships to human beings alone. The Psalms, Job, and Genesis are just a few of the books in the Hebrew Bible that place God in firm companionship with animals other than humans. Several chapters in the book of Job are particularly powerful exclamations of God's connection with the animals. God asks Job, "Is it by your wisdom that the hawk soars . . . Is it at your command that the eagle mounts up and makes its nest on high?" (39:26-27). Of course, the answer is no, rather it is God who gives wisdom to the hawk and commands the eagle. Even more explicit is the companionship God finds with massive animals, including Behemoth and Leviathan (whom some biblical scholars suggest might be symbolic of the hippopotamus and the whale).[39] These animals are inappropriate companions for humans, but God finds them glorious:

> Look at Behemoth, which I made just as I made you;
> It eats grass like an ox. Its strength is in its loins . . .
> It is the first of the great acts of God . . .
> Can you draw out Leviathan with a fishhook . . .
> Will it speak soft words to you?
> Will you play with it as with a bird,
> Or will you put it on a leash for your girls?
>   (Job 40:15–41:5)

It is almost as if God tells Job that Behemoth and Leviathan are akin to pets, even suggesting that God might put a leash on Leviathan much like a pet dog. They are God's alone, in a divine-creature relationship. In this companionship, God finds delight and intimacy, speaking softly and playing gently (as with a bird).

Second, now we know that humans have not been around for very long in comparison to the age of the universe, would it not stand to reason that God has been in relationship with the rest of creation since before we entered the scene? Again, biblical texts are full of hints that elaborate on this understanding of the divine. The Psalms tell us that God gives "drink to every wild animal" (104:11) and fills the sea with "creeping things innumerable" (104:25). In other words, much of the being of God is outside of relationship with human beings. God includes many other companion animals (and species). Some biblical writers and Christian theologians seem to have grasped this concept and provide us with a fascinating starting point.

Finally, as described by some intriguing Christian theologies of creation, God is actively looking for companions. God relishes in the beauty of the companion species created by and for Godself. In other words, God creates with companions in mind. As Carter Heyward, an Episcopal priest and professor of theology, states so eloquently, "In the beginning and in the end, God is a relation . . . the constant, immediate yearning and effort to make mutuality incarnate throughout the cosmos."[40] Heyward describes God as a verb, as the ground of mutual relationships. Terence Fretheim, professor of Old Testament at Luther Seminary, frames this idea of God in a slightly different way. The world of the Hebrew Bible, he suggests, is a "spiderweb of a world" with all of creation and God in these webs of connection.[41]

In addition to creation theologies, Trinitarian theology, a central concept of traditional Christianity, is inherently a companion theology. The Trinity is a relational God; it is God in companionship in various manifestations. God is Creator, Redeemer, Sustainer (or in more traditional language, Father, Son, and Holy Spirit). And all of these complex activities

are in relationship to each other. Pioneer theologian Sallie
McFague, one of my mentors, provides a provocative explanation of the Trinity, which she suggests has "been a source
of misunderstanding and mystification for most of Christian
history":

> As we are not solitary individuals, neither is God: in the
> ecological, economic worldview and in Christian faith,
> beings are individuals-in-community. We *are* because of
> relationships. The trinity, then, is not a conundrum or theo-
> retical obscurantism; rather it is the most basic affirmation
> we can make about God. The trinity is about relationship
> . . . the trinity is about God's love for the world and the
> world's response.[42]

So, within Christianity, God is understood as a God of companionship in complex and simple ways. This companionship is not limited to just human beings. Think about it—to
do so would be to limit God. And it would also limit us. If
the only companions deemed worthy of sacred or valuable
recognition are other humans, we are not only left with a
misunderstanding of who we are (since we do not and cannot
live in a one-species vacuum) but impoverished from the real
possibilities available to us in divinely given life.

Companion Animals in the Twenty-First Century: A Look at the Dog

*Cool Hand Luke is not going to die. I won't stand for it.
I know, of course, that he will, at least a part of me does.
After all, he's eleven, he's a dog . . . And I still love him so
deeply and completely that I imagine his death to be as if
all the oxygen in the air disappeared, and I was left to try
to survive without it.*

—*Patricia McConnell*[43]

Marc Bekoff, a biologist who spent years teaching at the University of Colorado, is, in my opinion, one of the most significant scientists of our time. Bekoff is an ethologist, an animal behaviorist. As his prestige and respect in the sciences grew, Bekoff began to focus on issues that are sometimes taboo among natural scientists. His vast research considers the possibility that other-than-human animals actually have compassion and empathy. Furthermore, he concludes that they develop a sense of justice, which he calls "wild justice." The consequence? Bekoff argues that we humans must reconsider our self-designated position of superiority. Working extensively with the renowned anthropologist Jane Goodall, Bekoff calls for compassion to and trust of the rest of the animal kingdom. In a powerful presentation he gave at the university where I teach, "Animal Passions and Beastly Virtues: Happy Hounds, Pissy Baboons, and Ecstatic Elephants," he made a strong case for animals having emotional lives—all based on scientific evidence. After carefully watching animals and recording their behaviors, the work of an ethologist, conclusions can be drawn and counted as part of the scientific method of inquiry.

Bekoff's work has made a huge difference in the consideration of the quality of life of companion animals. In a recent article, "Dog Trust," Bekoff defines what it means to "trust," a concept he relates to intention. He suggests that dogs have an "innate, ancestral, and deep faith in us," that they hold an "unwavering belief that we will take our responsibilities to them as seriously as we assume responsibility for other humans."[44] He follows this claim with a series of anecdotes about dogs, both dogs in situations where their trust in humans was well placed and dogs in situations where their trust was betrayed. As he writes, it is a "malicious double-cross to betray their deep feelings of trust in our having their best interests in mind" when we intentionally harm them, whether that be in a scientific experiment or by abandoning them at an animal control facility.

Dogs are, in Bekoff's opinion, "wonderful beings" who make us "more human." According to Bekoff, it would benefit humans as well as dogs if we openly "thank them for who they are, for the unfiltered love, and embrace their lessons in passion, compassion, devotion, respect, spirituality, and love."[45] This bridge to religion, to spirituality, is central to Bekoff's ideas about our relationship to other animals and, specifically here, to companion animals for whom we bear a different kind of responsibility.

In the United States millions of dogs live healthy and happy lives. At the same time, millions live in between, on chains in yards or banished to a backyard alone. And millions more die in animal control facilities each year because there are no homes for them. Statistics are difficult to verify since there is no central authority to gather data from the approximately 3,500 shelters in the country. *The best estimates project that six to eight million dogs and cats enter facilities each year in the U.S.; approximately half of these are euthanized.*[46] Amazingly, many people are unaware of how serious the pet overpopulation problem is in the United States. And it is difficult to imagine a Christian theology that would find such a situation acceptable. When a living, breathing, sentient being is born, God is on the side of life. Right? And yet the vast majority of the millions of faithful Christians in our country have no idea, allow it to continue, and all too often contribute to this horror themselves.

The stories of animal abuse are often too heartwrenching to share, but they are too numerous to ignore. The story of Freeway captures both the cruelty of some humans and the empathy of dogs. A call came into animal control late

Freeway, a three-legged dog rescued from the highway in Georgetown, Texas. Photo by author.

one night from a person who was on the interstate that cuts through the city of Georgetown. They had just witnessed someone throwing two dogs out of a truck. Both dogs were hit immediately by oncoming traffic on the congested highway. One dog, a black and white Australian shepherd mix, was moving around still, circling her companion and crying; but he had been hit too hard and was already dead. When animal control arrived they convinced her to come with them. Her rear leg was horribly injured. We took her into foster care and, after several failed attempts at surgery, we had to amputate her crushed leg. The pain must have been unbearable, but Freeway survived and is thriving on three legs. Granted, this story had a relatively happy ending for Freeway, though her companion died on the highway that night. How could someone throw two dogs out of a truck onto a busy interstate without even thinking twice about the consequences? Other stories of cruelty are even more direct and unimaginable to most of us. But we tend to ignore them or brush them aside because, after all, these are "only animals."

In my life I have been blessed with the presence and companionship of several wonderful dogs; I am grateful to my parents for introducing me to the beauty of living with companion animals. Fluffy Beauregard and Princess Magnolia (along with a cat, a bird, and several hamsters) grew up with me. When I was twenty-two and on my own in graduate school, I adopted my own pup. He was a scraggly little sick puppy hiding in the back of a cage at a packed, less-than-ideal animal control facility in Nashville, Tennessee. I had just learned that the old dog with whom I grew up, the magnificent Fluffus Beauregard, had died at the age of seventeen after a good life. A newly minted adult, I knew it was my turn to adopt my first dog. And there he was, a little white and black puffball that could fit in one of my hands. Though the staff person said he was six weeks old, Beaugart was probably only about four weeks old when I adopted him, way too young to be abandoned at an animal control facility all by himself and away from his mother.

Beaugart grew up to be a lovely border collie mix. He and I moved across the country together through two stretches of graduate school, a major personal life shift and new professional directions, and many difficult changes. He was my constant companion, the one who I knew would always be there, and I never, ever questioned his love. I hope he never questioned mine. I am now in my mid-forties, and Beaugart died after being with me for fifteen of those tumultuous years of early adulthood. When he died, my body literally ached. I went to the veterinarian whom I trusted very much and asked him to peacefully put my suffering friend to rest. I held Beaugart in my lap in the backseat of the car (he was scared to go inside), and Dr. Koy leaned across, comforting both of us to make sure that everyone was at peace with the next step in life. Beaugart rested, I said goodbye. It tore me in half.

Beaugart and I were companions in a relationship that I have no doubt was sacred. If anyone denies this, I will stand up and cite the most hopeful aspects of the history of the church and my understanding of God as a foundation to claim this calmly and surely: that God was made concrete in the relationship between Beaugart and me. With his death, I cried, I hurt, I grieved. But I would not have given up those years of companionship and joy for anything.

Though Beaugart passed away eight years ago, I still cry while I write this paragraph about him. Beaugart was my dear, dear friend. I will forever be thankful for and will forever miss his presence. Carter Heyward penned a lovely piece when her dog companion died, and it speaks to my sense of the life I shared with Beaugart as well. Whenever I read her reflection, I can still feel Beaugart's body, stretched across my lap, going to sleep for the final time. I believe it is this connection, this gift of enduring presence and love, that is sacred. In these relationships we find God.

> It was so hard and sad, holding you as you lay dying, my body pressed against
> yours, my hands kneading your warm, thick fur . . .
> You tucked your head beneath my stomach, your face into my left palm.

I rubbed your nose.
We breathed together in that awful moment, wanting so
badly, both of us,
to "go with"—the way we'd always done it:
the essence of your dogness, my humanness, our friendship
. . .
Could you tell how much I wanted it to be a gentle passage
for you, my beloved
friend?

> —Carter Heyward, *Journal*,
> qtd. in *Saving Jesus*, after the death
> of her dog, 1990[47]

Though many, and maybe all, domesticated animals had
some agency in becoming connected to humans, would any
compassionate person not acknowledge a certain amount of
responsibility for their well-being, now that they are solely in
our care? In the case of dogs, they rely on humans for food,
shelter, protection, and friendship. We rely on them for joy,
protection, assistance, and—also—friendship. And yet millions of them, every year, die unloved in shelters across our
country. Or, worse, suffer horrible abuses at the hands of the
humans who should be their caregivers. Surely the Christian
community, one called to compassion, to the reverence for
creation, and to the celebration of life, should be called to do
something about this as well. So how can individual Christians and communities of faith respond to the dire needs of
companion animals now?

As you saw earlier, the number of dogs killed each year
in the U.S. alone because there are simply not enough homes
for them is staggering. Some of this overpopulation problem
comes from the mass production of dogs as commodities by
"puppy mills." Puppy mills are large-scale, commercial dog
breeding facilities that approach these living beings as objects
to be sold for a profit. The state of Missouri alone has over

1,400 puppy mills, according to the United States Department of Agriculture. Other states, including Oklahoma, Kansas, Pennsylvania, Ohio, and Arkansas, are not far behind.[48]

Because laws in the U.S. offer little help in regulating these mass breeding operations, cruelty and neglect run rampant. Female dogs are bred repeatedly and kept in small kennels. Puppies are shipped nationwide to various retailers. Many of the puppies have health problems or are sold with paperwork that is falsified. Even though all of these claims might be disputed by the stores who sell the puppies, they have been well documented. In 2008 a bill dubbed the "Puppy Uniform Protection Statute (PUPS)" was introduced to both the U.S. House of Representatives and the Senate. At present, it is still in a committee and has not yet passed. Sometimes taking a public stance on an issue like this one can be controversial. But helping to end the cruel, profit-driven mass production of puppies undoubtedly falls under the umbrella of Christian compassion and reverence for life.

Rather than contributing to the exploitation of other animals just for the sake of financial gain, adopting pets from the overflowing shelters and rescue groups is a way to encourage life. There are amazing networks of people working with dogs and cats of all breeds, ages, and temperaments. Resources like Petfinder (http://www.petfinder.com/), through which over thirteen million pets have been adopted in fifteen years, are easy, accessible ways to find animals who need homes. Congregational facilities, usually with big parking lots, some shade, and great road frontage, are also good places to host adoption events for rescue groups and shelters. This is one direct way that the sacred relationships embodied in our companion animals can be affirmed.

In our houses of worship, furthermore, individuals can encourage a retrieval of some of the stories and studies of the texts that we discussed earlier in the chapter and seek other ways to bring nonhuman animals into sacred spaces. Through much of Christian history animals would have been wandering in and out of sanctuaries. Yet worship spaces eventually became fairly sterile and totally human centered. Most of the artwork with animals that used to adorn our worship spaces gradually disappeared. The scents and images were replaced by a focus just on the Word (a very human idea). Imagine how welcoming animals back in would change our awareness, and even more so, influence the spiritual and moral imaginations of our children.

As mentioned at the beginning of this chapter, some churches are carving out special worship times and places for people to bring dogs to church. As dogs become increasingly important companions for people who live without other humans in their households, this fills a gap in liturgy and simultaneously responds to a valid pastoral need.[49] Blessings of animals/pets that take place annually have already been growing by leaps and bounds, but certainly more congregations could add this to their calendar. Also, when a pet dies, recognizing the significance of that death with a memorial ritual would affirm the validity of grief at the loss of a valued companion.

These rituals have always been important for children. In a culture that hides actual human death (with the exception of television news and dramas), the death of a pet is often a child's first encounter with such drastic loss. Several months ago, my brother and sister-in-law's dog Hooker died after a wonderful life with them. Hooker was around nine years old and during their life together my two nephews entered the family. The whole family, mom, dad, and two sons, buried Hooker on their property. When I went to visit, my nephew Waylon, who was three at the time, took me to see the place where Hooker was buried. As we walked away from the gravesite, Waylon said, "I miss Hooker Aunt Laurie, it's sad." I replied with something I hardly recall now but let him know I was sad as well. Then Waylon said to me, "But it's OK because he's an angel in heaven who is still taking care of me." The loss is real, and we need to recognize it accordingly in our ritual, in our care, and in our friendships. I will come back to this theme in the final chapter of the book and also provide resources in the appendices for those interested in trying some of these new forms of worship.

What a friend we have . . . in companion animals, in our pets. Many human lives would be very lonely without them. Granted, in some ways they are a luxury, another mouth to feed and another medical bill to cover when there are so many humans who are suffering. This is true. But that also underestimates the possibilities for revealing God in these relationships. According to so many stories from the Bible and from the history of the church, God created a multitude of animals and takes pleasure in their company. Our lives are enriched immeasurably by the companionship of dogs, cats, birds, and other animals who live side by side with us day in and day out. Christianity has a word to say about this and calls us to provide for them with tenderness and responsibility. Surely Saint Martín of Porres, Saint Roch, Saint Gertrude, and Martin Luther would agree.

Chapter 2

Lions and Christians
Animals in Sport

Do you give the horse its might?
Do you clothe its neck with mane?
Do you make it leap like the locust?
Its majestic snorting is terrible.

—Job 39:19-20

My writing of this chapter began an hour after watching the beautiful filly Eight Belles give all that she had to the sport that caused her death. Eight Belles ran her heart out, coming in second out of twenty horses at the oldest sporting event in the United States, the Kentucky Derby.[1] This is a rare feat for any horse, much more so for a filly. The fillies are smaller, as females of many mammalian species are, so running competitively in a field of stallions is alone amazing. Nevertheless, this magnificent horse died as a result.

We humans have manipulated these fabulous animals, these equine symbols of strength, throughout much of human history. We ride them in battle and we position ourselves on them to show political and military prowess. Four of them even call forth the apocalypse in Christian Scripture. In recent years, however, we have changed their bodies so dramatically that at the end of the Kentucky Derby beautiful Eight Belles broke both of her front legs, a death sentence for any horse and certainly for a racing filly. Eight Belles was euthanized on the track within five minutes of the end of the race, after running the race of her life.

Paul Moran, a commentator for ESPN.com, observed, "When veterinarians reached the spot at which the gunmetal-grey filly lay motionless, there was no choice. Eight Belles was euthanized. Her heart had carried her to a place beyond where her legs were meant to go."

His analysis rings true on more levels than he might have imagined. Had her heart carried her there? Had her legs carried her there? Had her jockey and owner and breeder carried her there? This young girl was dead because we humans asked her to run as fast as she could on legs that could not do it. We have bred for speed and nothing more—and ask them to run at such a young age, before their bones are fully matured. Furthermore, we likely push them to their limits by injecting them with performance-enhancing supplements like steroids.

At the end of her ordeal, her visibly distressed trainer Larry Jones had this to say:

> She ran the race of her life. We were through racing; all we had to do was come home. There's a reason for everything, but I see no reason for this. The main thing is that she didn't suffer. She went out in a blaze of glory . . . Losing an animal like this . . . I don't know what to say.[2]

This issue is far bigger than this one trainer and this one horse, and I do not want to lay blame at the foot of this man who clearly had compassion for his horse. However, why do we humans not know what to say in such an instance? Where were Eight Belles' legs meant to go? We figured out a way to force them to go somewhere else, somewhere that her bones and muscles could not reach. And can we really say to ourselves that she didn't suffer? She died quickly, yes. But for a few agonizing minutes she must have suffered. And, moreover, her life ended when she was a child, with only three of potentially thirty years of life lived.

We use them—animals—for sport, for leisure, for entertainment, for financial gain. Two years before the Eight Belles tragedy in 2008, the renowned stallion Barbaro won the Kentucky Derby. The entire nation waited anxiously for him to win the Triple Crown. No horse has done that for three decades. Then, leaving the gate at the Preakness Stakes, the second leg of the three-race series, his leg broke. Together we slowly watched the tragedy of Barbaro's death unfold. It took months. Veterinarians worked on him. People worldwide prayed and mourned and . . . he died.[3] Could Eight Belles and Barbaro be two of the four horses of the apocalypse? Could they hail our demise, reminding us that not only have we made them fragile but, in so doing, we have made ourselves fragile as well?[4]

Since the earliest days of Christianity and before, sport that involved the bodies of "others," a complicated category of those both human and animal thought to be expendable, was central to many dominant cultures, including those of the Mediterranean world. Some generalizations about such sports are part of popular Christian legend. We hear about "throwing Christians to the lions," but the entire story is much more complicated. The dominant members of these societies would select those who were exploitable and expendable and put them into the gladiatorial arena for entertainment. In the first several centuries of the Common Era, as Christianity was growing slowly throughout the Roman world, those who chose this new religion often faced death alongside animals.

Though very troubling, reading some of the accounts of Christians and the animals with whom they shared the Roman arenas provides a helpful lens for considering animals and sport in the contemporary world. There are several other important junctures in history, including nineteenth-century England, when Christianity and animals in sport once again intersect. These episodes of connection raise questions of how Christians in the contemporary world might respond to how animals are used for sport and entertainment in dominant and even mainstream human culture. In studying these episodes, can one find anything that Christianity has to say about the ethics of using animals for entertaining humans?

Throughout human history we find examples of entertainment or sport at the cost of other lives—sometimes other human lives, but often other animal lives.[5] How does this loss of life, this cost of life, for the purpose of entertaining those privileged enough to participate as safe spectators, or as powerful contestants (the ones with the weapons, for example), fit in Christianity? After watching the majestic and beautiful Barbaro and Eight Belles die so tragically and being reminded so strongly of Job 39:19-20, I am convinced these questions must be seriously considered.

There are a number of "sports" that involve animals. I chose only three for the focus of this chapter—thoroughbred horse racing, dogfighting, and trophy hunting. All three are "blood sports," and self-designate as such, so that moniker is not to be read as a derogatory category into which I have placed them. Thoroughbred horse racing is a blood sport in a different way, on some levels, since it relies on the "blood" of the animals to make sure they are, indeed, bred thoroughly (from specific lines). Dogfighting and trophy hunting rely on blood being shed for the "sport" to be successful, at least from the perspective of the humans involved. These blood sports are particularly appropriate ones for Christians to consider, as for three centuries Christians were the objects of such sport themselves in the Roman Empire.[6]

Throwing Christians to the Lions

*And Thecla . . . was stripped and received a girdle and
was thrown into the arena. And lions and bears were let
loose upon her. And a fierce lioness ran up and lay down
at her feet. And the multitude of the women cried aloud.
And a bear ran upon her, but the lioness went to meet it
and tore the bear to pieces. And again a lion that had been
trained to fight against men, which belonged to Alexander,
ran upon her. And the lioness, encountering the lion, was
killed along with it. And the women cried the more since
the lioness, her protector, was dead.*

—Acts of Paul

Thecla was a virgin companion of Paul the Apostle during his journeys. In the apocryphal *Acts of Paul* she shares the limelight in the accounts of his life. The passage above is one of several relating what happened with Thecla and "beasts" in Roman arenas.[7] In her book *Animals in the Apocryphal Acts of the Apostles*, Janet Spittler details various accounts from the Roman era of lions befriending humans, particularly females.[8] As Spittler points out, Thecla's faith allowed her to escape death a number of times. The theme of the "beasts" responding to her recurs frequently when she is captured and becomes part of the spectacle of the games. For instance, elsewhere in the apocryphal *Acts of Paul*, Thecla was bound between two bulls, "red-hot irons" were placed "under their genitals so that they, being rendered more furious, might kill her."[9] At this point another divine intervention burned the ropes that tied her to the bulls, and she stood in the arena unharmed.

The games of the Roman Empire were clearly dangerous places for humans and for animals. They followed a fairly standard pattern, with animal hunts (*venationes*), followed by executions (Christians would have been part of this entertaining display among other criminals and captives), then finally the gladiatorial fights. Sometimes these different stages would be conflated, so animal fights and executions of criminals could happen simultaneously. A number of stories tell of animals sent out to attack Christians.

However, while early Christian history is replete with stories of martyrs, particularly of those killed by the Roman Empire for refusing to sacrifice to the state, if sheer numbers are any indication it was likely safer to be a Christian in the Roman system of games than to be an animal. According to a variety of sources, a vast number of animals were killed as the empire displayed its wealth and power. Animals were imported from throughout the growing Roman territories in order to astonish the citizens with these exotic prizes. As the games grew in importance, so did the number of animals killed for this violent sporting enterprise. Elephants, leopards, lions, crocodiles, and even the occasional hippopotamus, sometimes considered among the spoils of war, were used in the games to please the crowds and instill a sense of the dominance of the emperor and of Rome itself. If Rome could capture these majestic beasts while defeating people throughout the world, then it went without saying that the Empire was terrible and mighty.

As the games progressed through the centuries, an increasing number of animals were killed as each emperor would outdo his predecessors. So, while Marcus Scaurus boasted of a *venatio* that included 150 leopards and five crocodiles in 58 B.C.E., Pompey's games in 55 B.C.E., a mere three years later, "included the slaughter of 20 elephants, 600 lions, 410 leopards, various apes, the first north-European lynx to be seen at Rome, and the first rhinoceros."[10] By the time of the dedication of the massive Colosseum in Rome in 81 C.E., the stakes had risen significantly and the emperor Titus presided over the death of at least *nine thousand* animals during the inaugural games. (The slaughter continued in the year 107 C.E. after the emperor Trajan won a military victory and Rome celebrated with 120 days of events. Reports indicate that *eleven thousand* animals were killed during this stretch of entertaining games.[11]) J. M. C. Toynbee, one of the first modern art historians to examine animals in the Roman world, writes that the "numbers of animals slaughtered on specific occasion are recorded cold-bloodedly and, indeed, as a matter for congratulation." Her list of these recordings is powerful and covers the chronological escalation of violence. Toynbee seemingly caps her account with the "animal holocausts" of Domitian, also well-known for his early persecutions of Christians, who "is said to have slain with arrows 100 wild beasts of different kinds on his Alban estate." But then even Domitian is surpassed:

> Trajan, however, beat the record by the butchery of 11,000 beasts to celebrate his Dacian triumph. But for refinement of cruelty to animals Commodus took the palm. He kept animals at home in order to kill them: in public he dispatched with his own hands 100 bears, 6 hippopotamuses, 3 elephants, rhinoceroses, a tiger and a giraffe; and according to Herodian, who also mentions lions and leopards as Commodus' victims, he shot ostriches with crescent-shaped arrowheads devised to decapitate the birds, whose headless bodies went on running.[12]

There was little mercy, and apparently much bloodlust, for animals in these Roman games.

Inscriptions from cities like Pompeii served as advertisements to lure crowds to the games. Some of these inscriptions listed the animals in a hierarchy of dangerousness: "four days of games at Beneventum starred . . . wild cats, sixteen bears, four other dangerous animals the rest being herbivores." Even those animals who were no threat to humans were slaughtered: "and you yourselves remember, excellent citizens, that on each of the four days all the herbivores were killed."[13] In addition, mosaics throughout the Roman world depicted the hunts and the circus scenes with animals fighting each other and fighting the gladiators.

While numerous Roman sources brag about the animals killed in the games, early Christian texts also provide interesting accounts of the animals as well as the humans. Not only were many executions performed *ad bestias* (with the condemned being thrown to the wild beasts), but, according to early Christian sources, sometimes the executions did not end as planned. At times the "beasts" (lions, boars, bulls) did kill the Christians, now martyred in the games. But there were also incidents when *ad bestias* backfired and the wild animals *refused* to kill the Christians. Reminiscent of Daniel in the lions' den, the animals instead offered up their own lives in defiance of the Roman masters.

Texts in the apocryphal New Testament, particularly those focusing on the lives of the apostles, include fascinating stories of animals in the arenas who seemingly recognize and cooperate with these early Christians. The story of Thecla, mentioned above from *Acts of Paul*, is among several in that text alone. One of the most powerful encounters is between Paul and a lion. Paul was in Ephesus and had been arrested. The governor asked the crowd what to do with him and the crowd answered (as was expected), "To the beasts with this man!" So Hieronymus, the governor, made "a display of animals," including a lion who roared so loudly that even Paul "broke off his prayer in terror." The citizens of Ephesus, always ready for the games, began to cry out at dawn, "Let us go to the spectacle! Come, let us see the man who possesses God fighting with the beasts!" Then an interesting twist changed the anticipated scene completely. Rather than attacking and killing Paul, the lion gazed at him with recognition. Earlier in their lives, they had encountered each other, and the lion had requested that Paul baptize him. Now, both prisoners of Rome, they met again in the arena. The baptized lion will not attack Paul. Hieronymus decides to send other beasts and even archers to kill both Paul and the Christian lion. To save the two faithful victims from the Roman onslaught, God intervened and sent a mighty hailstorm. Paul and the lion escaped from the arena and, both now fugitives, went on their way—Paul on a ship and the lion into the wilderness.[14]

Other martyrologies abound that report encounters between Christians and animals in the arena. Seemingly divine intervention or communication with the animals is sometimes implied, as in this account reported by the early church historian Eusebius:

Again you would have seen others—there were five altogether—thrown to an infuriated bull. When others approached from outside he tossed them with his horns into the air and mangled them, leaving them to be picked up half-dead; but when in his fury he rushed head down at the long group of holy martyrs, he could not even get near them, but stamped his feet and pushed with his horns in all directions.[15]

The infuriated bull might easily have been another one who was subjected to torture in order that he might be angered. In the case of Blandina, a slave who was one of the martyrs of Lyon in the late second century, Eusebius writes that she was "hung on a post and exposed as food for the wild beasts let loose in the arena." Eventually, however, since "none of the beasts had yet touched her," she was removed and "kept for a second ordeal."[16]

Of course, in addition to the stories of animals who befriend or at least refuse to kill Christians, there are reports of "wild animals" or "beasts" killing them as well. Many of these are deaths welcomed by the human martyrs. Ignatius, a first-century bishop of Antioch whose iconography depicts him being eaten by a lion, states in one of his letters, "May it be for my good that the wild animals are ready for me . . . I shall coax them to devour me promptly, unlike some whom they have been afraid to touch."[17]

Tertullian, one of the early Fathers of the church, is the likely recorder of an account of the martyrdoms of Perpetua, a young noblewoman, and her servant, Felicitas. These two women were martyred in the year 203 C.E. in Carthage. Theirs is arguably one of the most significant stories of martyrdom from the first three centuries of Christianity. Just before she was imprisoned, Perpetua gave birth to a son who she "suckled" and then "commended" to the care of her mother and brother. Felicitas was herself pregnant when she and Perpetua were apprehended and was greatly relieved when she gave birth early. "Pregnant women are not allowed to be publicly punished," and Felicitas longed to be martyred at the same time as the other prisoners. When the two women were taken into the arena, "stripped and clothed with nets," the crowd "shuddered as they saw one young woman of delicate frame and another with breasts still dropping from her recent childbirth." A "fierce cow" was sent out to attack them "for that purpose contrary to custom, rivaling their sex also in that of the beasts."[18] In order to humiliate the prisoners completely, the cow was sent rather than the bull as a way of taunting the women.

It is striking to compare this account of Perpetua and Felicitas, with its focus on them as mothers who recently gave birth, to an account recorded by Martial, a first-century Roman poet who described the opening games of the Colosseum in his work *De spectaculis liber*. He describes the death of a pregnant pig who was "stabbed with a spear" before giving birth:

> Nor did the piglet lie still; instead, as its mother fell, it ran away . . . At one and the same time, the sow lost life and gave life . . . By her fatal wound she became a mother. O, how ingenious are sudden and unexpected events.[19]

While the crowd is seemingly entertained by the mother and tragically orphaned baby pig it is shocked by the human women who recently gave birth. At least there is some sense of dismay expressed at the death of the two human mothers, but the crowd seems to have no sympathy for the sow.

Interestingly, even contemporary observers drew connections between different aspects of the games, as evidenced by an announcement found at Pompeii that promised the crowds "crucifixions along with animal hunts and gladiator duels."[20] The series of events were all part of the same gathering, whether it was the execution of a human on a crucifix or the death of an animal in a duel. Christians in the arena were killed parallel to the myriad animals, both humans and animals sacrificed for the entertainment of the human crowds.

With this history in mind, it seems appropriate for Christianity to consider the state of animals as part of the sports-entertainment system of the contemporary world. Dominant cultures, those with power, use the "other" in order to amuse. The shared history of Christians and other animals in the games of the Roman Empire gives new meaning to the idea of "throwing Christians to the lions," since, by all accounts, the lions were as likely to be victims of that system as the Christians. If we are serious in following Paul's lead, then, perhaps the lion should also be freed from the abusive power.

Case 1: Thoroughbred Horse Racing

As a child I met the most noble, the largest, the most beautiful creature I still have ever seen. I was a lucky little girl who had family in Kentucky, and they took me to Claiborne Farm to meet the retired, mighty "Big Red"—Secretariat. If I close my eyes today, I can still see him standing next to me and towering over everyone. He had intense but sweet eyes. Secretariat loved to run. They all do. Horses thrive on running. Whether or not horses love to run is not the question in thoroughbred horse racing. The problem is with the conditions under which they are compelled to run: their physical makeup, their genetics, and the pressure imposed on their bodies by their owners and trainers, as well as by all the spectators and gamblers.

If one considers the overall numbers, it might seem that relatively few horses die racing. According to the Associated Press, five thousand racehorses died between 2003 and 2008 in the United States.[21] In comparison, in 2005 alone over 91,000 horses were slaughtered for food for either human consumption or for the pet food industry.[22] In general, because thoroughbred horses garner heavy financial investments from some quite wealthy human beings, they are more valuable alive than dead. But the numbers are still staggering, and they were difficult for the Associated Press to gather. As

Author with Secretariat in 1979, Claiborne Farm, Paris, Kentucky.

a matter of fact, many states and racetracks do not even keep the statistics on thoroughbreds who die either on the race-track or as a result of racing injuries. It is not much of a leap to assume that 5,000 is a conservative number at best. And this is to say nothing of what happens to these horses after their racing careers end, as we will discuss later.

Horse racing has ancient roots, possibly dating as early as the seventh century B.C.E. Xenophon (c. 430–335 B.C.E.), a contemporary of Socrates, wrote *The Art of Horsemanship* over 2,400 years ago, and it is still in print.[23] In addition to the many games discussed above, Roman chariot races were a central part of their games; the horses used for these races, though occasionally sacrificed by the winning team as a way to thank the gods, were highly sought after. Thoroughbred horse racing in its relatively modern form began after the Civil War, though it has roots before that in England, and has always been tied closely to the gambling, or gaming, industries. Winning purses of over $1 million are seen with frequency in the major races; the owners of Mine That Bird, the winner of the 2009 Kentucky Derby, took home over $1.4 million.

Many familiar with the sport agree that horses die on the racetracks too often. On June 4, 2009, *The New York Times* reported that, "Since the beginning of the year, 20 racehorses have been euthanized after breakdowns in racing or training accidents at Belmont Park or Aqueduct."[24] The magazine *Blood-Horse*, one of the major reporting tools of the thoroughbred racing industry, reported that the National Thoroughbred Racing Association recognizes it to be problematic that the "horseracing industry had no systematic program for collecting data on equine injuries or fatalities at racetracks."[25]

While millions of dollars are invested annually by veterinary schools and the horse racing industry to improve the physical characteristics of these horses, speed is always the primary factor in the selection of horses for breeding and racing. Is this selection process detrimental to the overall health of thoroughbred horses? Some evidence points to that possibility. First, most thoroughbreds weigh over

1,000 pounds but have ankles the size of those carrying a human who weighs under 200 pounds. Second, the genetic pool is sometimes questioned as well. Studies conducted on 500,000 thoroughbreds show that in "95% of these modern racehorses, the Y-chromosome can be traced back to a single stallion—the Darley Arabian, born in 1700." This genetic pool carries certain defects and, according to Matthew Binns of the Royal Veterinary College in London, "One tenth of thoroughbreds suffer orthopaedic problems and fractures, 10% have low fertility, 5% have abnormally small hearts and the majority suffer bleeding in the lungs."[26]

Even the most accomplished thoroughbred racing horses can have tragic deaths. A famous case is that of Exceller, a horse who won seven major races and even defeated two Triple Crown winners. Exceller earned over $1.6 million in races, and upon becoming a stud his breeding fee was $50,000. Unfortunately his offspring did not fare well, and his fee declined significantly. He was sold to a Swedish breeder who eventually declared bankruptcy and slaughtered Exceller in 1997.[27] We should also remember Ferdinand, the winner of the 1986 Kentucky Derby. Initially retired to Claiborne Farms, the same farm where I met Secretariat, Ferdinand also had an unsuccessful stud career and was eventually sold to a company in Japan. According to *Blood-Horse*, Ferdinand is believed to have been slaughtered for pet food in 2002.[28] The huge public outcry following his death led to the introduction of the American Horse Slaughter Prevention Act in the U.S. Congress, which passed in 2006. While this legislation closed down the last remaining horse slaughter operations in the U.S., it is still possible for horses to be shipped from the U.S. to Canada and Mexico for slaughter there.

Thoroughbred horse racing raises the issue of human dominion over animals in ways that, at first glance, are not always obvious. Horses have been used as draft animals to pull plows for agriculture. They have been used as pack animals to carry our loads. They have provided transportation for generations and still do today. Examining horses' lives in all of these settings is certainly valid. The well-known and treasured novel *Black Beauty*, written by Mary Sewell in 1877 in response to the abuse of cab horses in Great Britain, is one of the early modern calls to humans to treat horses with dignity and compassion. However, the purpose of using thoroughbred horses for racing points to an extreme situation as we humans manipulate, slaughter, and ride these animals, sometimes to their deaths, simply for the purpose of sport and gambling.

On May 17, 2009, Rachel Alexandra, another fabulous filly like Eight Belles, won the Preakness Stakes. The huge television and live audiences seemed to share a collective sigh of relief after she completed the race uninjured. Just two weeks earlier, eight bells tolled at Churchill Downs, the site of the Kentucky Derby, in tribute to the filly who died there on that day the year before. And, on the day following the 2009 Kentucky Derby, the mantle of roses won by Mine That Bird hung over the neck of the new statue of Barbaro, the only horse buried on the grounds of the famous track. The inscription under Barbaro's status quotes Eric Liddell, the 1924 Olympic Gold Medal winner: "I believe God made me for a purpose, but he also made me fast. And when I run, I feel his pleasure." Surely Barbaro and the many other horses who have died on the thoroughbred racing tracks loved to run, but their bodies were pushed too hard and manipulated too drastically by humans for them to fill this God-given purpose.

Case 2: Dogfighting

In April 2007, police raided a now-infamous property in Surry County, Virginia, uncovering evidence of a dogfighting ring. In June, federal authorities entered the property and found sixty-six dogs, mostly pit bulls, being used for dogfighting. Dogfighting is a widespread "sport" in the United States and one that has a long and graphic history in other parts of the world as well. The owner of this property—Atlanta Falcons superstar quarterback Michael Vick. The descriptions of the scene are beyond chilling, and because media jumped on the story this horrific sport has finally reached much of the public's awareness. For those who did not hear details of the story, witnesses to the events that took place on Vick's property describe dogs being killed by "hanging, drowning, and/or slamming" them to the ground if they did not perform well in testing sessions.[29] They were coldly executed, forced to breed in order to perfect the fighting drive, and made to fight to the death.

While the disturbing and horrifying scene in southern Virginia on Vick's property captured the news media's attention in 2007, dogfighting was not and is not limited to that one well-known, celebrity-focused incident. After the Vick case, in July 2009 the biggest dogfighting raid in U.S. history took place, with 450 dogs seized across eight states and human perpetrators arrested in several of these raids as well. According to prosecutors in Missouri, members of this multistate dogfighting ring killed injured dogs by shooting them "in the head, throwing the dogs into the river or burning the dogs in a barrel."[30] This coordinated effort between law enforcement and humane organizations focused on the widespread illegal and violent activities associated with dogfighting. As Scotlund Haisley, senior director for Emergency Services of the Humane Society of the United States (HSUS), reported,

After months of coordination and preparation, the sweet
release of relief is finally beginning to wash over our
exhausted team. This feeling is ushered in by the comforting sight of dogs being settled in at the emergency shelter.
Knowing that without our intervention these same animals would have faced a future of untold horrors is my
ultimate reward. Tonight I can truly celebrate a belated
Independence Day, as I contemplate the 450 lives that have
been saved from the clutches of the dogfighting industry.
By shutting down these operations we have saved untold
generations of fighting dogs the pain and misery of being
bred only to quench the blood lust of those involved in this
hideous industry.[31]

As discussed in chapter 1, for hundreds of years dogs and
humans have lived together in close relationships and companionship, two species in interesting symbiotic concert for
at least 15,000 years. But evidence suggests for at least the
last *two thousand* years dogs have been used not only to protect humans and their property but, for a variety of human-
centered reasons, to fight other animals, including other dogs.
The Roman Empire's use of animals opens a window into
this early history of dogs fighting, guarding, and engaging in
other violent acts at the command of the humans with whom
they live. The mastiff breeds, likely emerging from the culture
of the Greek and Roman empires, are still central to dogfighting, as it is one of their remote descendants, the pit bull,
that has become the victim of choice in the contemporary
dogfighting world. Dogfighting is not unique to the Mediterranean and European cultures, however. There is a history of
this particular blood sport in areas of eastern Asia and South
America as well.

The particular type of dogfighting taking place in America in the early twenty-first century, however, has a more
recent history of development. Starting in sixteenth-century

England, dogs were used as part of a growing interest in "baiting" sports. Large animals, such as bulls or bears, would be chained or otherwise weakened, and powerful dogs would be loosed to attack them. Often these fights would take place in a "pit," a type of fighting ring for the animals. And from there was derived the name of the primary type of dog used in fighting in America, the "pit" bull terriers.[32] In the first half of the nineteenth century in England, baiting became illegal, so the fights were staged between two dogs rather than between a dog and another, larger animal. In the twentieth century, in rural, urban, northern, and southern areas of the United States, dogfighting emerged as a major component of gambling cultures.

While dogfighting is illegal in all fifty states and it is a felony in most states, it has rarely been pursued and prosecuted, as is evidenced by the existence of an official publication serving the interests of the dogfighting community: the *Pit Bull Reporter*. The *Pit Bull Reporter* offers this description of the American pit bull terrier (APBT):

> The fact is no other breed has the gameness or ability to consistently stand up to the APBT in an even weight fighting contest. (You may have heard of a pit bull losing an occasional street or backyard fight against this breed or that but we are talking about "professionally conducted" pit matches in this context. Poorly bred, amateurishly handled pit bulls may lose to another breed once in awhile, just as a sorry horse may lose a race to a mule occasionally . . .).[33]

Breeding operations for pit bulls are widespread, and the names of many of these operations leave little to the imagination about the violence inherent in their programs: Bad Newz Kennels, Dead Man Kennels, Short Fuse Bulldogs, Terminator Kennels, Armageddon Kennels, and Silent But Violent Kennels.[34]

A number of arguments propose that dogfighting is a particularly masculine sport. In a recent article in a gender studies journal, sociologists argued that their research "confirms that the dogs employed in the sport of dogfighting do serve as symbols for the traditional masculine ideal of heroism that exists within the subculture of dogfighters and they are the symbols through which their owners gain status as men." Further, dogs who lose the fight or who refuse to fight are condemned and often killed by their owners if they have not already been killed in the pit. As one dogfighter stated, "If the dog is capable of standing on his feet, he should keep fighting and never quit, I would condemn any dog that chooses to quit."[35]

For a moment, let us put aside concerns for animal welfare and consider the other alarms raised here. Even if one is only concerned with human welfare or if one worries that concern for animals might lessen one's concern for humans, issues of animal abuse and violence to other humans are closely connected. Numerous studies in recent years demonstrate the links between domestic violence and animal abuse as well as between dogfighting and violence toward other humans. Researchers consistently see support for what is called the "graduation hypothesis" of the animal abuse-human violence equation. In short the "perpetrations of acts of violence toward animals may desensitize the perpetrator to the effects of violence, as well as reinforce violence as an effective means of social control."[36] The links between domestic violence and animal abuse are increasingly obvious, according to a number of sociological studies.[37] The more likely one is to abuse an animal, the more likely one is to abuse one's spouse, partner, or children.

Humans and dogs have lived together for tens of thousands of years. Controversial and compelling theories about how and why this relationship came about proliferate. But one thing is irrefutable: dogs have a unique place in human lives. The fact that many humans can enjoy torturing them in pits for sport and gambling reveals the human capacity for cruelty and evil. Randy Grim, a dog rescue worker in Saint Louis, describes the fate of the many of these dogs, particularly the ones who are not the winning fighters. He had rescued one of them and describes him here:

> The golden Chow, the dogs in the woods, and the black dog curled up in the backseat weren't fighting dogs, not successful ones anyway. They were either discarded losers or leftover bait. He'd rescued a lot of dogs that had been used as bait: the starving, yellow Lab-shepherd mix chained and mutilated in a yard where a healthy Pit Bull roamed free; puppies skinned alive near a crack house on the East Side; the terrier mix with ribbonlike scars up and down his front legs from the wire used to tie him down.[38]

Grim's account is eerily similar to the reports from the raid on Vick's property and from the various raids in July 2009 when over four hundred dogs were confiscated.

As I mentioned above, the pit bull is not a breed but a confusing categorization of a particular appearance. Unfortunately, for the dogs so labeled, the classification can be a death sentence. A number of U.S. cities have banned pit bulls, and increasingly, homeowners' insurance providers will not cover these dogs in policies. For renters, landlords who allow other pets will not allow "pits" in properties. At the shelter where I volunteer in central Texas, the most common "breed" confiscated, surrendered, or found stray is the pit bull. Because of the stereotypes associated with them and the associated breed-specific regulations that unfairly burden them, it is difficult to get these dogs out of the shelter into new homes or into rescue groups. But I see their

*"Sheba" was a pit bull who ended up at the Georgetown Animal
Shelter. She had likely been used as a bait dog for fighting practice.
She was missing one eye, and there were tears in both of her ears.
Photo by Jimmy Smith.*

faces all the time and have encountered numerous gentle,
people-loving "pits" over the last decade. A colleague and I
get as many of them out into foster homes as possible. But
we never are able to bring enough to safety. However, we
did get "Sheba" out.[39]

Sheba was a small, brindle female who obviously had
been used for breeding and, likely, also used as a bait dog. Her

left eye was missing and she was full of worms (heartworms, hookworms, whipworms). Several chunks of each of her ears had been bitten off. She shivered in the corner of her run and hid her head in my lap when I sat down next to her. It took a few months of good food, veterinary care, and the experience of kind humans, but I will never forget the first time I saw her wag her tail. Suddenly Sheba realized that life was OK. She simply wanted to live, she did not want to fight. During several months in one of our wonderful foster homes, she was spayed, she was treated for heartworms and the many other parasites that filled her body, she gained weight, and her coat started to shine. She and the woman who adopted her bonded immediately. This story had a happy ending.

Too few former fighting, breeding, and bait dogs realize the same happy ending, though. Many of the dogs seized from Vick's property were placed with Best Friends Animal Sanctuary in Utah. This well-established, experienced organization worked diligently with these dogs to rehabilitate them and placed most of them in good homes. Some of these former fighting dogs are still at Best Friends over a year later and could end up spending their lives at this sanctuary. But the dogs from the huge raid of July 2009 will likely not be as lucky. It is incredibly difficult to find appropriate homes for dogs who are traumatized. While the HSUS, Best Friends, BAD RAP, and other organizations do everything they can to determine the best final outcome for dogs who were used in dogfighting operations, many will never be saved.[40]

Sport Hunting

During the latter half of the seventh century, in the wilderness of southern France, lived Saint Giles, a "hermit known for his holiness" and for his healing miracles who chose to reside in a cave away from other humans. According to his hagiographies, or stories of his life,[41] the saint was befriended and fed by a doe. She would come and nourish the saint with her milk. Because of this doe, we can learn much about what the stories of Saint Giles have to say about hunting for sport. Most people living in the early Middle Ages hunted for at least some of their food, and the nobility of the time had the luxury of hunting for entertainment as well. The wealthy citizens claimed certain areas of land exclusively for the purpose of sport hunting. The hagiography tells the story of Saint Giles and the doe:

> The king's men came hunting in that area and saw the doe. Caring nothing for other game, they pursued her with their dogs, and the doe, hard pressed, took refuge at her foster's feet. Giles wondered why the animal was whining and whimpering, which was not at all like her, so he went out, and, hearing the hunt, prayed the Lord to save the nurse he had provided. No dog dared come closer than a stone's throw, and the pack returned to the huntsmen barking and howling vehemently. Night drew on and the hunt turned for home. They came back the next day, but their labors were thwarted again, and they returned home as before.

At this point in the story, the hunters are clearly looking for this specific animal, not for animals to kill for food. Unsuccessful in their attempts to kill her, they are accompanied by the king when they resume their hunt the next day. Eventually they surround the cave where the doe is hiding with the saint. The story continues:

> One of them incautiously shot an arrow, hoping to drive out the quarry, but instead inflicted a serious wound on the man of God as he prayed for his doe . . . [T]hey found the old man wearing a monk's habit, white-haired, venerable with age, and the doe stretched out at his feet.[42]

This Christian saint, Giles, not only provided refuge for this doe but took an arrow for her to save her from the sport hunters.[43]

Hunting holds a traditional and powerful place in many cultures; it is usually more than a way to gather food.[44] Historically, sustenance hunting has been central to human survival and has been accompanied by rituals and symbolic layers too complicated to address here. Social class issues, such as those hinted at in the story of Saint Giles, are only one of many levels of meaning attached to hunting. Humans are omnivores. We can eat a wide variety of plants and animals. True, some argue against this designation and point to religious and environmental reasons for humans to be vegetarians; however, that is an issue addressed more fully in chapter 3. But let us grant here that humans are omnivores. Does that still mean that hunting for sport rather than sustenance is in line with Christian ideals? It is this category of hunting that the story of Saint Giles, and possibly other ideas from Christianity, calls into question.

Hunting is a way of life for many people; it is a tradition that has been handed down from one generation to another. Certainly there are hunters whose primary purpose is gathering food, and while various arguments can be forwarded in support of or against this, that is not my goal. It could be argued, and validly in my opinion, that careful hunting for meat is preferable to buying meat at a grocery store, since that meat likely came from a factory farm (an issue addressed in chapter 4).[45] But sport hunting focuses on trophies, on entertainment, on killing for the purpose of killing, not for survival, not for food. Just as dogfighting provides entertainment and is acceptable in some subcultures, hunting for sport is not only acceptable but expected in certain U.S. subcultures. And often in the same communities where hunting for sport thrives, Christianity thrives as well. Because of this link, it is imperative for Christians to think about the implications of faith on sport hunting.

Here is an interesting experience: do an Internet search for "hunting" and "Christianity." You will be surprised by how many connections are made between the two. One of the most intriguing is Outreach Outdoors, a "Christian Hunting Ministry." Almost every person listed on the biography of the website page is pictured holding up the head of a dead deer by his antlers, presumably a buck they recently killed. There is a "harvest" page as well, featuring images of deer, mostly bucks with large antlers, dead on the ground with their heads held up by the hunters. Interspersed are night-vision pictures of deer still alive. In the descriptions of the "harvests," they graphically describe the deaths of the deer: how long they survived, which way they ran after being shot or hit with an arrow. Still, according to their literature, "God wants to use hunting" in order "to draw people to Him." And this is the purpose of the Christian hunting ministry.[46]

Matthew Scully, a senior speechwriter for President George W. Bush, published *Dominion* in 2002. The second chapter of this book, "The Shooting Field," paints a picture of sport hunting in the United States. Scully spends the first part of the chapter describing his experience at the seventh annual convention of Safari Club International. There are exhibition booths with vendors selling exotic hunting trips, award ceremonies for those who killed certain combinations of animals, and seminars on a variety of topics from "African Bowhunting Adventures" to "Wild Game and Wine Pairing." And later in the chapter he describes one of the traditions of the convention:

> It is the Christian Sportsmen's Fellowship breakfast . . .
> The fellowship's motto is "On Target to Catch Men for

Christ." Their logo depicts a deer head beneath a cross. About 250 people are here. There is a raffle: hanging in the balance, a camouflage-covered Bible.

Scully continues his description with a quotation from the main speaker at the event, a former governor, ex-president of the National Rifle Association (NRA), and Medal of Honor recipient, Joe Foss. Foss explains his understanding of the connections between Christianity and hunting:

> And that's why SCI (Safari Club International) is so impor-
> tant, because it protects our right to hunt . . . You have to
> say, "Lord Jesus, come into my life, forgive my sins" . . . If
> you have the Lord on your side, you'll win. If you don't,
> you lose. And hunting and fishing—if you're involved in
> that, it's tough to go wrong . . . I believe in the Bible and
> everything in it . . . Every human being is a miracle. It's hard
> to believe—there are so many of us—but it's true. Think
> about it. A miracle, the world created for you. You're it.[47]

So it seems hunting, as understood by the Christian Sports-man's Fellowship, is a sacred expression of the mastery that we have over the world. But did God create the world just for us—the miracle humans?

A search through their website provides some more insight into the group's overall mission. The pictures at the top of the front page include a rifle with a scope, a fishing rod, a mounted fish, a bear, and a buck (the last two are still alive in the images). On the "Mission" page their vision state-ment begins with a quotation from Psalms 42:1: "As the deer pants for streams of water, so my soul pants for you, O God." In juxtaposition, the "Photo Gallery" page contains images of dead deer in the hands of hunters.[48] While many of these hunters are likely not "trophy or sport hunters" exclusively (they probably do eat the meat, though they may mount the heads of the bucks), the presentation of the animal whom they just killed is certainly a trophy moment.

Today, in this country, exotic trophy hunters spend thousands of dollars to kill animals on designated hunting ranches. Driving around the barely suburban and rural roads of central Texas, game fences run along the edge frequently. On one of those ranches, for example, you can spend $4,500 for a five-day aoudad hunt; the aoudad is a Barbary sheep species native to North Africa but now, apparently, roaming the not-so-open areas of central Texas for sport hunting. An hour north of Houston, hunting for a zebra will cost you $6,500, for a wildebeest, $4,500. A third ranch advertises a bongo hunt for $35,000; this is particularly noteworthy since the bongo, the largest African forest antelope, is on the *threatened species list.*[49]

In his book *Without a Tear*, ethicist Mark Bernstein describes a moral principle that he dubs the Principle of Gratuitous Suffering (PGS): "It is morally wrong to intentionally inflict (or allow the infliction of) gratuitous pain or suffering on another, innocent individual."[50] This may seem like a less-than-groundbreaking moral statement, but if we took it seriously, think of the difference it would make. In light of the PGS, Bernstein examines hunting. He places it squarely in the middle of the dialog of "sport," as hunters frequently refer to themselves as "sportsmen" or "sportswomen." His insights here are provocative, and they apply not only to hunting but to dogfighting and horse racing as well.

> Sporting events involve voluntary participants. All the parties have some chance of winning, with the winner typically rewarded with money, a trophy, or a medal. But hunting has none of these characteristics. Obviously the animals do not voluntarily enter the sport. No doubt, given the chance, the deer, squirrel, or dove would opt out of the event. Nor

> does the animal have any chance of "winning." The best
> outcome is to leave the arena a free, uninjured creature.[51]

Indeed, maybe that is the best outcome for the animals in each of these blood sports.

In his article "Unsportsmanlike Conduct" in *Christian Century*, Dean Peerman suggests that while hunting per se might not be contradictory for Christians, canned hunting for sport is. Peerman points out that the animals on the exotic hunting ranches are often raised with humans, therefore tame and unafraid. He even references occasions when animals on these ranches will lick the hand of the hunter before being killed. In response to an article published in *Christian Century* in support of hunting, Peerman states that Christians should "disapprove of" canned hunts.[52] The display of violence for entertainment and to show power over another should ring a bell for Christians. This was the idea behind crucifixion in the Roman Empire.

Christian Responses to Animals in Sport

I began this chapter with a description of the powerful filly Eight Belles and the image of her front legs breaking after she ran majestically in a race. Horses, dogs, and trophy animals are among those who die at the hands of humans engaged in "sports." In much the same way, early Christians sometimes died at the hands of Romans for entertainment.

Christians have not been entirely silent on these or very similar issues over the course of the last two thousand years. While sources are somewhat scattered, there is a rich history of critique of this unnecessary violence and suffering. I simply offer a sampling of these voices here and leave a more in-depth analysis of conclusions for the final chapter.

The first critique is found in canonical Scripture itself. In Matthew 12:11 a man with a withered hand was in the

synagogue, and the people with Jesus asked him if it was law-
ful to cure on the Sabbath. Jesus responds to them, "Suppose
one of you has only one sheep and it falls into a pit on the
Sabbath; will you not lay hold of it and lift it out? Imagine
Jesus' words in relation to dogfighting when dogs are thrown
into a "pit" together to fight until one can no longer stand
and is most likely dead. Here, not only does Jesus tell his
disciples to pull the sheep out of the pit, but he tells them
they can break the laws of the Sabbath in order to do so. Is
it unreasonable to think that Jesus would expect compassion
for our animal companions?

In his seminal work *Utopia*, written in the early sixteenth
century, Sir Thomas More, a devout Catholic and adviser to
Henry VIII, provided a vision of a tolerant, peaceful world.
In his description, he takes on the issue of hunting. More
states that Utopians "think that this whole business of hunting is beneath the dignity of free men . . . [T]he hunter seeks
nothing but pleasure from murdering a poor innocent beast."
More does assume that there will be butchers to provide meat
for the population, but the culture of hunting is what is at
issue for him. Furthermore, in Utopia they "never sacrifice
any animals, for they can't imagine a merciful God enjoying
slaughter and bloodshed. They say God gave His creatures
life, because He wanted them to live."[53]

In the 1650s when the Puritans took control of England
following the Elizabethan era, as part of their overall restruc-
turing of English culture they eliminated the blood-sporting
Cotswold Games. The Puritans had a different "sporting
ideal" than that of their predecessors. The Cotswold Games
included "blood sports or butchery sports often centered on
animals pitted against each other in barbaric contests to the
death. Bear-baiting, bull-baiting, dog-fighting, and cockfighting were commonplace and drew audiences from all ranks."

The Puritans sought to replace these blood sports with "wholesome, clean, non-violent" athletic competition.[54]

For a variety of complex historical reasons, Evangelicals in England contributed significantly to the discourse on the humane treatment of animals beginning in the nineteenth century. This is perhaps surprising to some Christians. The conclusions the Evangelicals drew about humanity's relationship to animals were informed both by classism and, naturally from their perspective, a certainty that Christian culture was the only true and right way to live. As such, it would be an incomplete picture to remove issues of racism, classism, and sexism from these stages in the development of the humane movement as a whole.[55] Still, there are points about the situation of animals from their perspective that remain helpful in the ethical and moral consideration of blood sports.

First, the Society for the Prevention of Cruelty to Animals (SPCA) was officially launched in 1824, followed by several other societies that would provide the foundation for the animal protection movement.[56] Their earliest focus was bull-baiting and cockfighting. These people continued their efforts into other arenas, such as draft animals and companion animals, but their initial reaction was to these sports. A significant number of their most influential members were evangelical Christians. For example, William Wilberforce,[57] a member of Parliament and of the Clapham Evangelicals, provided one of the strongest voices in opposition to animal baiting fights:

> When we considered that the victim of this human amusement was not left to the free exertion of his natural powers, but bound to a stake, and baited with animals instinctively his foes, and urged by acclamation to attack him, must we not conclude that the practice was inconsistent with every manly principle, cruel in its designs, and cowardly in its

execution? . . . On a comparison of the different sports, it would be found that none of them partook of cruelty so largely as bull-baiting.[58]

Wilberforce was not alone in his denouncements. Preachers such as Reverend Styles, who was a committee member for the SPCA, declared in 1835,

> I should repudiate Christianity if it circumscribed our sympathy. But far different is that spirit of mercy, which "wipes all tears from all faces," and enjoins us to turn out of the path lest we "needlessly set foot upon a worm" . . . Christianity is no indifferent spectator of animals suffering, but the stern avenger of the wrongs of that defenceless race which cannot defend themselves.[59]

Various articles published in *The Evangelical Magazine and Missionary Chronicle* in the early nineteenth century encourage Christians to consider animal welfare. In December 1834 the magazine published an article entitled "On Cruelty to Animals," which declared,

> Should any affirm that they nevertheless enjoy it, let them turn to our bull-baits, our badger-hunts, our multitudinous and multifarious sports, in few or any of which can it be adduced that cruelty to the subordinate animals does not form a prominent feature. Morally, socially, and above all, religiously, we sin deeply in thus causing unnecessary suffering.[60]

The direct engagement of Evangelical Christianity with blood sports in the nineteenth century provides a wealth of resources to ponder in the early twenty-first century as well.

Numerous contemporary Christian theologians, from Carol Adams to Andrew Linzey to Jay McDaniel, have much to say about cruelty to animals as well, and their works are cited throughout this book. In addition, there are continuing links between Christianity, humane organizations, and the issue of cruelty to animals in the world of sport. The HSUS is, in many ways, a direct descendant of the nineteenth-century British anticruelty societies. While the direct links to Christianity and the overt connections with Evangelicalism are certainly not apparent, the HSUS increasingly makes connections with religious communities from all traditions to address issues of animal cruelty.[61]

Nevertheless, despite these efforts, early twenty-first-century American culture continues to support a world of cruelty in sport, and as mentioned earlier, this violence does not just involve animals but certain human "others" as well. Watching those who are not "like us" fight to the death, die at the other end of a weapon we wield, or exert themselves to a point that leads to death is in many ways reminiscent of the lives of the early Christian martyrs. In the Roman world, they were the "other," the expendable ones whose suffering was valid for entertainment purposes. After gaining power and influence, however, Christianity slipped too easily into making "others" of its own, and into using "them" for similar purposes.

Still the roots of compassion in Christianity run deep. From images of Jesus healing those who most people would not touch, to Francis of Assisi negotiating for the wolf to live peacefully in the town of Gubbio, to Mother Teresa providing health care for the "others" of Calcutta, Christianity has a rich tradition of bridging the gap and extending a hand of compassion. Surely, as we have seen over and over again, that compassion need not stop with humans.

Chapter 3

Eating Mercifully
Animals for Food

All animals live in contentment and serve God,
loving and praising Him.
Only the evil, villainous eye of man is never satisfied . . .

—*Martin Luther* [1]

I grew up an urban child with the occasional summer visit to my great-grandfather's farm in Tennessee. That was the first place I held baby pigs and rubbed the noses of cows. Those cows would "hightail it" when we put out special food for them, and I learned that it really did mean they held their tails high in the air as they came happily running across the pasture for a treat. We would squirt milk from the cows' udders into the mouths of the barn kittens and get fresh water from the spring. To me, obviously, this was a magical place with so many animals happily living on a family farm. Certainly there was a side to this that I might have missed, but it was the same picture that is so often drawn to mind in popular culture (and portrayed in advertising) of happy cows and hens living in green pastures before they come to market as food.

However, one year when my parents decided to save some money by purchasing a side of beef directly from a church friend, my image of cows on the farm dramatically changed. On this trip out to the country—made to finalize the plans for the side of beef (which as a twelve-year-old I later realized was a different way of saying half of a dead cow)—I stood at the fence looking at these yearlings. The rancher pointed to one of them, one who looked so young to me, and she told my parents that was our cow (well, half of him). Unfortunately for my mother (who had difficulty getting me to eat that cow), my own eyes had already connected with his big brown ones. To this day, over three decades later, I can still see those eyes. It was the first time I wondered whom I was eating.

In the United States, and much of the Western world, the twentieth century witnessed a great distancing of humans from the food we eat. Most humans in the U.S. live far from our food—both vegetable and animal. It is shipped from country to country, it is processed, it is packaged, it is placed on store shelves. On many levels this is an unsustainable food practice; one need only read Michael Pollan, Barbara Kingsolver, or Alisa Smith and J. B. MacKinnon to get a sense of the urgency of addressing our current food production and distribution system. And for the animals who become meat, this food system has become increasingly cruel.

Everyone eats. We die if we do not. So it makes sense that one of the central features of religion is food. It is obvious if you think about it. Religion helps explain who we are. We cannot exist—we cannot *be*—if we do not eat. Food is central to our lives and our deaths, ergo food is central to religion. It is not a stretch to claim that food is the foundation of human culture.[2] Food is still loaded with meaning, even though in the contemporary world it seems to be very secular in nature.

Food defines cultures and identifies people as insiders or outsiders, and as such its impact on religion cannot be underestimated. So where does food and what we eat fit into the complicated history of Christianity? How might this inform our food choices in the twenty-first century? From the apple in the garden of Eden to the bread Jesus broke with his disciples, Christian stories are full of food.

Food as Ritual and Practice in Christian History

God's original plan was to hang out in a garden with some naked vegetarians.[3]

After planting a vegetable and herb garden on the campus to try to learn how to grow their own food and to contribute to a more sustainable food production system, some of my undergraduate religion and environmental studies majors started to ponder more broadly how religious ideas influence what and how they eat. The bumper sticker quoted above, which they enthusiastically presented to my department, seemed to capture some of their questions—and also some of their initial conclusions. Does God intend Christians to be vegetarians? What instructions does the faith have to offer?

The history of food and Christianity is so rich and full of resources that in such a short space it is almost impossible to begin a discussion of this topic. What follows is just a very brief overview so that we may later consider a contemporary response to meat-eating practices. It you want to read more, which I encourage you to do, delve in to some of the resources in the recommended reading list at the back of this book.

Eating and Animals in the Scriptures

In tracing the resources provided by Scripture, where else to begin but in the book of Genesis, where in the first chapter food is already addressed. Genesis 1:29-30 tells that God

gives humans and other animals "every plant yielding seed
that is upon the face of all the earth, and every tree with
seed in its fruit; you shall have them for food. And to every
beast of the earth, and to every bird of the air; and to everything that creeps on the earth, everything that has the breath
of life, I have given every green plant for food." Paradise is
a wonderful image of peaceful cohabitation (remember, all
naked vegetarians), with all of the beasts of the earth and
birds of the air, indeed with every being that has the "breath
of life," eating the green plants and fruit, but not eating
each other. Humans and all of the other animals are in the
same general category, which is utterly distinct from God; all
have "breath" and live together peacefully. Indeed the text
does say that humans are the ones created in the image of
the divine and have a special place in the creation, but God
restricts everyone's diet.

However, between the fall, when humans first eat a forbidden food, and the flood, the relationship between humans
and what we eat takes a dramatic turn. In Genesis 9 the flood
has just ended and God is giving instructions to Noah and his
family. Reflecting back on the ideal state pictured in Genesis 1,
God says to the people, "the fear of you and the dread of you
shall be upon every beast of the earth, and upon every bird of
the air, upon everything that creeps on the ground and all the
fish of the sea . . . Every living thing shall be food for you; and
as I gave you the green plants, I give you everything." What a
drastic change in the human-animal relationship in just eight
chapters! And a bizarre conclusion to a story that included
all of these animals rescued from the deluge. After the flood,
humans are "feared" and "dreaded," quite a different picture
than the one of peace and harmony portrayed at the beginning of creation. Humans are now given all the animals to eat
(though this will be clarified and restricted again), but only

in a tense relationship of fear and dread. Does it not sound a bit like a curse?

Throughout the Hebrew Bible from then on, food becomes central as God lays out the rules around what to eat, how to eat, and with whom one should eat. These eating regulations are central to the laws of Moses, which guide the lives of the Israelites from that point forward. Animals must be slaughtered a certain way, with their blood offered as a sacrifice to God in order to alleviate the guilt of the humans who have, literally, murdered these animals. Additionally, not all animals can be consumed. There is actually still a modified vegetarian ethic in place. Leviticus 11 gives a complete list of which animals are clean and which are unclean. The basic division, though this is not the formal reason given, identifies "clean" (thus edible) animals as those who are herbivores. So the Israelites are not allowed to eat animals who eat animals. Pork is forbidden, since pigs are omnivores; birds of prey—eagles, vultures, ospreys, buzzards—are also "detestable" as food.[4]

God also challenges the Israelites to share food, provide for those who might otherwise go hungry—the poor, the widow, the orphan—and to never forget that they were once slaves in Egypt (Exodus 24). This position of justice, demonstrated in the sharing of food, extends throughout both Testaments of the Bible; for example, in 1 Corinthians 11 Paul criticizes those who partake of the Lord's Supper while others in the community go hungry. And the limits of generosity with food are extended to other animals. One particularly powerful story in Genesis 24 lays out the importance of sharing the well water with camels.[5] Indeed, numerous texts relate God's generosity with food for all of God's creatures, not just humans. Psalm 104 praises God for causing "the grass to grow for the cattle" and giving the lions their prey.

As one enters into the New Testament, one can see that nascent Christianity adopts some of these ideas as well, particularly those directing believers to share food with each other. The most commonly cited passage is the miraculous feeding of the multitudes, one of the few stories common to all four canonical Gospels (Mark 6:30-44, Matthew 14:13-21, Luke 9:10-17, John 6:1-15). While various interpretations can be gleaned from these accounts, all focus on the necessity to feed everyone who is present. Jesus also reminds his followers that God provides for all of the creatures, including the birds who live in the branches of the mustard plant and the sparrows who fall from the sky.

In general, though, Christianity seems to move away from a strict dietary code and from the laws that regulate how one can slaughter animals. As early Christianity begins to separate from Judaism and to shift its message to include Gentiles, many of the dietary markers that provide identity for Jews are abandoned. The voices of Paul and his closest followers apparently take the lead in this process. In the Letter to the Romans, arguably the most influential of his Epistles, Paul declares that those "who eat must not despise those who abstain, and those who abstain must not pass judgment on those who eat; for God has welcomed them" (14:3). The context here is extremely important, since Paul was attempting to unite Jews and Gentiles into a new religious community; thus he tried to minimize conflicts over differing practices.

Just as images of an idyllic paradise are present in the creation stories in Genesis, images of the end times, the kingdom of God on earth, often include the peaceful coexistence of all of God's creatures. The most significant prophetic passages are Isaiah 11:6-8 and Romans 8:18-23. In Isaiah a series of animals who are usually fearful of each other, indeed one is often food for the other, dwell together peacefully—the wolf and the lamb, the calf and the lion—and a "little child" leads them. Certainly, the little child could also be food or at least be in danger, since the passage says that the child can play over the nest of the dangerous snakes. Paul's description of salvation is more general, but it also spells out redemption for "the whole creation," not just for humans. With a focus here on food, though, the implications of the Isaiah passage, when put into dialogue with Genesis 1, are striking. Images of the peaceful coexistence of animals who would otherwise eat each other define paradise in Scripture.

Food in Christian Worship Rituals

Food holds a prominent place in Scripture. So, obviously, it holds a central place in many Christian rituals, and it is paramount to the most basic and powerful one. While not the case for all Christians, most forms of Christianity agree on two foundational sacraments—baptism and the Eucharist. In the spectrum of Christian traditions, the forms of these two rituals shift significantly throughout Christian history. Among Christian communities, however, water is almost always the basic element of baptism, and food is always the focal point of the Eucharist. Sometimes called Communion or the Lord's Supper, the Eucharist centers on grapes in the form of juice or wine and grains in different bread incarnations. These basic food groups—fruit and grains—are then shared by those gathered. While it is rarely conceived as "food" specifically, rather as a symbolic or memorial or miraculous substance, the Eucharist is, nonetheless, a food ritual.

The Eucharist emerges from a long and complex history of its own. Generally understood to be connected to the Jewish Passover, the Eucharist also seems to be related to early Christian agape meals, or love feasts. Sacrificial rites involving various animals, most often the sacrificial lamb, may provide some of the foundation as well. A number of studies have been written from both a liturgical and a sociological perspective to further explain how it developed in early Christianity.[6] But most agree that the *Didache*, a late first- or early second-century Christian catechesis or teaching text, provides the earliest reference to the Eucharist or "Thanksgiving Meal." The *Didache* describes the cup and the broken bread and stipulates that nobody can partake of the Eucharist if they are not baptized. By the end of the first century of Christianity, a ritual meal or feast is a well-established part of Christian gatherings.

Why bread and wine? In his fascinating study *Ascetic Eucharists*, Andrew McGowan reveals that in some early Christian communities bread and *water* were frequently used rather than bread and *wine*. Still others used bread alone. Was this simply a matter of convenience or economics? McGowan suggests it was not—though certainly bread and water were staples of the Mediterranean diet, particularly the diet for the less powerful members of society. Rather, these food choices were intentional responses to the Roman sacrificial system. The choice of bread as the central "food" for the Christian ritual provided a reproach to the empire's animal sacrifices—the only source of meat for many. Some of the earliest evidence of Christian opposition to animal sacrifice is found in Paul's First Letter to the Corinthians. Paul was deeply engaged in discussions surrounding the eating of sacrificial meat, an important matter and cause for significant disagreement among early Christians in Corinth and beyond. But Paul likely shifted the perspective to a symbolic one.

In addition, Paul moved the followers of this new movement away from the restrictive dietary practices of Judaism, including those that emphasized humane slaughter and prohibitions of eating certain animals. In other words, Paul opens up the world of meat eating to Christians. But this does not seem to be the case with the stories about Jesus. While many stories are told of Jesus feasting, the only meat we hear about him eating is fish, and that only rarely. Rather he emphasizes the feast of bread and wine in all of the canonical Gospels. This "shared meal" practice that is a central feature of the stories of Jesus continued to develop in the tradition in the form of love feasts, which I sometimes think of as a first-century potluck meal, and the "vegetarian" Eucharist.

When Christians gather around tables each Sunday, or in many cases more frequently than that, to celebrate this sacred meal, food is there front and center. Whether the bread is understood as transforming miraculously into or being symbolic of the body of Christ and the wine into his blood, the grain and grapes on the table are being blessed, shared, consumed, and recognized as sacred. Sometimes the bread is leavened, sometimes not; sometimes the grapes are fermented, others times not. There may be no cup offered at all, only bread. In each tradition the specific types of food used in the Eucharist are important—as they mattered to early Christians who gathered for this ritual and, it seems, for an entire shared meal.

But do we find food elsewhere in Christian ritual? Is food truly central to the faith? If so, what does the tradition have to say about our food choices today? As a basic element of life, food also provides a window into many cultural symbols and systems. The examples listed below are not a complete listing by any means, but rather a representative look into how food is part of Christian life, in both a practical and a symbolic way.

First, consider the Christian ascetics. Seeking spiritual strength through the intentional practice of a rigorous and disciplined life, ascetics have held a consistent, continual and important place through all of Christian history. Some argue that it was John the Baptist who first set the pattern for the many Christian ascetics who followed him. Two of the earliest were Saint Mary of Egypt and Saint Symeon Stylites. They, along with other desert dwellers, lived in a tense relationship with food—simultaneously understanding it to be both a gift from God and the temptation into evil, just as the apple was for Adam and Eve. In an attempt to cleanse their bodies and, for some, to deny their bodies, many of these early ascetics chose to eat so little that they barely survived. Later ascetics include the well-known and now-beloved Saint Francis of Assisi and Saint Catherine of Siena. Both of these medieval mystics bordered on starvation at times during their lives due to their complete religious devotion. Fasting, for most of these ascetics, was not an end in itself. Rather it provided a way to tame desires, to focus on prayer, and to connect with others through the compassion fasting generated.

Francis of Assisi is the patron saint of ecology and is also closely associated with the blessings of animals. Francis is likely the most well-known and popular saint in Christian history. Numerous stories from his life (some of which are told in other chapters) tell of his close relationships with other animals. He praises a cricket for her devotion to early morning prayer, preaches to birds, and saves a wolf from the wrath of a local village. As mentioned in chapter 1, the most common day for congregations to hold blessings of animals is the feast day of Saint Francis on October 4.

In the earliest version of Francis' "Rule," basically the way that the brothers joining his order were instructed to live, Francis states that "all brothers should fast from the feast of All Saints until Christmas, and from the Epiphany, when Our Lord Jesus Christ began to fast, until Easter."[7] He also includes all Fridays as days of fasting. This might seem like quite an extended period for limited eating, but one must keep in mind that Francis espoused the life of a beggar, so food was an uncertain commodity for him and his followers. However, it was not unusual for Christian religious orders in the Middle Ages to observe such intense regimens of eating discipline.

But Saint Francis was not the only ascetic to have a special relationship with animals. Read also about Saint Anthony Abbot, the patron saint of animals. Often accompanied by a pig in his iconography, Saint Anthony lived in the late third and early fourth centuries and is generally regarded as the founder of Christian monasticism. The stories about him tell of Anthony searching in the wilderness for another early Christian holy man, Paul the Hermit. After finding him, Anthony discovers that Paul subsists on the piece of bread he receives each day from a raven. This meager diet fed Paul for years. Saint Anthony, whose life story was told most powerfully by Athanasius, proved one of the most influential figures in Christian history. He ate bread and salt, drank water, and spent his life in prayer.

In her powerful and complex study of the lives of medieval women, Caroline Walker Bynum explains that food is, crossculturally, a particular concern for women, who are often the preparers of it but not as often its consumers. In this context, a fascinating pattern develops in the stories of medieval Christian holy *women* as they abstained from food themselves but shared food with others. Like Anthony, Francis, and Paul, they also sought a closer relationship with God through their eating practices; sometimes these holy women would eat nothing but the Eucharist for days or months. Consider Bynum's description of Colette of Corbie, a fifteenth-century hermit and member of the Poor Clares, the female Franciscan order:[8]

> Colette supposedly began to fast as a child, giving away
> her dinner to other schoolchildren, running from the fam-
> ily table to welcome beggars at the door and press them to
> accept her food. From girlhood she ate no meat . . . More-
> over she effected cures with food, putting bread she had
> chewed into the mouths of two sick sisters or, on another
> occasion, curing with a crumb of bread.[9]

The famous historical saints are just the tip of the iceberg, as millions of Christians have, over the course of its two-thousand-year history, practiced various forms of asceticism, and most, if not all, of these forms include special attention to what one eats. In the early and medieval church, and to a certain extent into the modern period, fasting has been a practice for all Christians, not just for members of religious orders or those who practice various forms of asceticism. Fasting is a concept and practice closely related to the Eucharist. The Eucharist, by design, is the *feast* which follows the *fast*. For many Christians in the Roman Catholic tradition still today, a fast is observed throughout the day until the Eucharist is received. Even more prominent are the communal fasts that take place during the season of Lent, the forty days preceding Easter. For generations, believers prepared for Easter, the great Feast of the Resurrection, with a series of devotional practices that included special attention to food. In the Western church, the forty days of fasting began with Ash Wednesday and were kept Mondays through Saturdays (only Sundays were exempt from fasting). No meat was eaten, especially not on Friday. This was in recognition of the traditional remembrance of Jesus' crucifixion on Good Friday. Early church fathers from Tertullian to Clement of Alexandria emphasized the potential of fasting as a religious discipline. And, as Pope Gregory the Great wrote of Lent to Saint Augustine of Canterbury in the late sixth century, "We abstain from flesh, meat, and from all things that come from flesh, as milk, cheese and eggs." The truly devout would limit themselves by eating no animal products and often eating just one small meal per day. Eventually, not wanting to miss an opportunity for a party, Christians started to celebrate Fat Tuesday, or Mardi Gras, on the day before Ash Wednesday. We still see examples of this pre-Lenten celebration of eating and drinking (heavily) across the globe. But Lent throughout Christian history was taken seriously, and the role of food in it was no small matter.

Today, Christians are mostly just vaguely aware of the widespread practices of fasting that are part of the liturgical seasons of Christianity. Yes, we see signs for the Friday "fish fry" in front of Catholic churches now, held so that parish-ioners and others in the community can abstain from other meat on these days during Lent. Many Christians "give up something" for Lent, though it is usually chocolate or baked goods or some other minor or indulgent category of food. The idea of abstaining from all "animal products" during Lent has not been followed widely for at least a generation or more in the Catholic Church and rarely if ever in Protestant communions. However, for at least fifteen hundred years, abstaining from eating animal products during Lent was a sign of respect, penance, and devotion. Fasting—as a prepa-ration for the Eucharistic feast and as a way of practicing religious discipline—was central to Christian life.

Second, consider an entirely different Christian food ritual, one firmly rooted in U.S. Protestant Christianity: the potluck dinner. If you were raised Protestant in America in the twentieth century, you more than likely attended your fair share of fellowship suppers or potluck meals at church. In both mainline white Protestant churches and African Ameri-can churches, the communal sharing and enjoying of food is a central part of church life. From the early nineteenth-century camp meeting gatherings through the late twentieth-century doughnut spreads before Sunday morning worship, to the sharing of meals during fellowship hour in the African Methodist Episcopal Zion churches, Protestants come together over communal, social meals. "Coffee hour" followed the Sunday morning worship, and it became standard practice for the Baptists and the Methodists to race to the local restaurant to beat the crowd for the post-worship meal gathering. In my childhood church, we actually had a Sunday school "kitchen class" where the members gathered in the sacred space of the kitchen to swap stories and prepare for coffee hour. It was one of the two or three most important spaces in the church and one that still evokes fond memories from me.

In their fascinating study "There's Nothing Like Church Food," Jualynne Dodson and Cheryl Townsend Gilkes describe the significance of food in the black church. They write, "Food is a central part of the African American Christian experience. It is taken very seriously in both positive and negative ways. It is sung about. It is worried over. It is prayed over. It is the subject of church meetings." Food is a means of sharing, of remembering, of building solidarity, and of recognizing the importance of being embodied. The kitchen itself even becomes a place full of religious life, with some people remaining in the kitchen to prepare meals during the worship service while listening to the service over loudspeakers. Banquets and feasts—for ordinations to Pentecost birthday parties to fund-raising events—are hallmarks of the community.

Another study, wittily titled *Whitebread Protestants*, looks at food in the various dominantly white churches in America. In it Daniel Sack writes, "church food is far more than a menu and a place. It is community."[10] He explores the extended impact of food and religion on each other in this particular slice of culture. Food becomes a central avenue for mission and outreach as churches organize food drives or develop soup kitchens in economically distressed areas. Many churches become the central point of organization and delivery for Meals on Wheels. Many others collect food for international aid repositories. And churches rally around the cry to end global hunger. Sack concludes that Christians take seriously the idea that Jesus was made known to his disciples after the resurrection through breaking bread (Luke 24:35). Whether in the form of a potluck or an outreach drive, churches break bread together and build community over and over again.

In truth, it would take volumes to examine all of the connections between Christianity and food over the last two thousand years. From the earliest days of the tradition, Christians gathered to share love feasts and a ritual of memory; debates ensued over what to eat and when to fast; members of religious orders chose strict diets and ascetics ate little if anything in order to discipline themselves; twentieth-century American Protestants, in their many forms, gathered for potlucks and tried to share food on a global scale. But the point, I hope, is clear: Christianity and food are intricately connected. Christianity knows the importance of food. And w*hat a Christian eats is a religious subject.* So, in the twenty-first century, how might Christianity approach this central issue?

Eating Animals in America: The Bleak Reality of Factory Farming

Imagine a row of light pink-white sows standing inside metal crates that measure five feet long by two feet wide. In these cramped enclosures, little piglets walk around their mothers on the metal barred floors. The mother pigs do not have room to turn around, just to lie down so the piglets can nurse.

The grated floors allow excrement to pass through. A person scoops some corn into a small opening in the front of the crate. There is one small, vented window; no other windows are in sight. This was the photo accompanying a newspaper article entitled "Old Hands Help Aspiring Farmers Put Down Roots" in the Sunday edition of the *Austin American-Statesman*, my local newspaper, August 16, 2009. Written by an Associated Press journalist, this piece was published in a variety of newspapers across the U.S.

I was amazed at the matter-of-fact nature of the picture of this factory farm. Would no one be shocked by this image? It was as if the writer assumed that no one would question the normality of the horrible life that these mother and baby pigs were living. Has this unnatural reality become accepted as normal? Pigs: confined in small crates with no fresh air, no sunlight. Dirt and mud to wallow in replaced by metal grates. The article was about trying to encourage people to return to the "family farm," but the image that accompanied the story was evocative of anything but the idyllic family farm.

In a course I teach on religion and ecology, my students watch the documentary *Baraka*, a compelling film that analyzes through images the sometimes chaotic nature of modern life (there are no words, just music to accompany these images). One series of scenes shows thousands of small yellow balls of fuzz being zipped around a factory's whirlwind of conveyor belts. Some are picked up by factory workers, cursorily examined, and either returned to the belt or thrown into a chute leading to a trash bin. The ones left on the conveyer belt head to a bright, obviously red-hot plate, which they are held against for about two seconds. Then they all tumble together into bins and are moved along. These small yellow balls are chicks being prepared to be either "broilers" or "layers." They are debeaked because the conditions under which they are kept are so tight and stressful that they will peck away at each other and at themselves. If the factory is looking for egg layers, the males are discarded and left to suffocate piled on top of each other in a trash bin. My students are, understandably, always disturbed by the scene: cute little chicks tossed, burned, trashed, and traumatized. They are treated as mere objects, not living beings; in the modern factory farming system these chicks (and the cows, pigs, lambs, and other animals born to be food) are mere commodities on the conveyor belt of mass production.

Industrialized factory farming is a hidden reality of the shift in the U.S. diet, a shift that has seen Americans eating ever-increasing amounts of meat. According to statistics provided by the United States Department of Agriculture (USDA), meat eating escalated dramatically in the last fifty years. In 2007 over ten billion (10,000,000,000) animals were killed for food in the United States alone, *almost forty animals per person*. The chart below illustrates the general increase, over 50 percent more than per capita consumption in 1950:

Year	Meat Intake Average in Pounds Per Person
1950	144
1960	161
1970	189
1980	190
1990	193
2000	211
2007	222

Chickens on a truck. Photo © Shutterstock.

The major jump is in the number of chickens consumed. In 1950 the average person consumed 21 pounds of chicken per year; by 2007 that increased to 87 pounds per year.[11] How can we possibly supply this amount of meat for over 300 million people? It requires slaughtering a daunting number of animals. According to the USDA, on one day, October 2, 2008, 126,000 cattle, 432,000 hogs, and 4,000 calves were slaughtered in the U.S. alone.[12] The statistics for chickens are even more startling: 9,075,261,000 (over nine billion) slaughtered in the U.S. in 2008.[13] In the United States, we are fed by a mass production system comprised not of farms but factories.

How pervasive is this system in American food production? In his study on the transformation of the rural landscape in the U.S., *Empty Pastures*, Terence Centner provides the following statistics. Since 1960 "hog farms have decreased by 92 percent; farms with dairy cows by 93 percent; poultry operations, by 71 percent; and cattle operations, by 55 percent."[14] When those statistics are placed next to the numbers indicating an astounding increase in the amount of meat consumed per capita, not to mention the increase in population overall, it is apparent that more and more animals are being raised on significantly fewer and fewer farms. Thus, these animals are much more concentrated. According to the Environmental Protection Agency, there are approximately 17,000 large confined animal feeding operations (CAFOs) in the United States.[15] What does this mean in terms of sheer numbers of animals on any one CAFO? A few examples suffice to give a sense of the size of these operations:

Animal	Size threshold (number of animals) for classification as a "large CAFO" by the EPA
Cattle or cow/calf pair	1,000 or more
Swine (weighing less than 50 lbs.)	10,000 or more
Chickens other than laying hens	125,000 or more
Laying hens	82,000 or more[16]

Some states bear the brunt of this concentration. For example, in Arkansas an average poultry farm has 274,839 birds.[17] North Carolina and Iowa have large concentrations of pigs, while California has by far the most dairy cattle, an interesting shift from the days of Wisconsin cheese. Texas, where I live, was "home" to 14.1 million beef cattle in 2006, and the number of dairy cattle is rising dramatically as other states institute more stringent regulations because of the waste products.[18]

Though public awareness of the food system is beginning to grow, many Americans remain completely unaware of how our meat is produced. And the impact of these operations is widespread, far beyond the problems of animal welfare. In April 2008, after two and a half years of investigation, the independent Pew Commission on Industrial Farm Animal Production (PCIFAP) released a report on the effect of CAFOs.[19] The commission examined several areas, including impact on public health, the environment, animal welfare, and the health of rural America. Though the focus in this book is on animal welfare, one needs also to note the adverse community health effects on humans from CAFOs that are recognized even by the Centers for Disease Control (CDC). The CDC states that

> [p]eople who work with livestock may develop adverse health effects, including chronic and acute respiratory illnesses and musculoskeletal injuries, and may be exposed to infections that travel from animals to humans. Residents in areas surrounding CAFOs report nuisances, such as odor and flies. In studies of CAFOs, CDC has shown that chemical and infectious compounds from swine and poultry waste are able to migrate into soil and water near CAFOs.[20]

And these chronic conditions do not even start to address the diseases that can pass from animal to human and are much more likely to emerge from such crowded conditions.[21] On March 7, 2003, an article in the magazine *Science* reported on an outbreak of flu at a North Carolina pig factory in August 1998. At first some pigs started coughing, and within short order, every one of the 2,400 pigs broke out with flu symptoms, including high fever, lethargy, and poor appetite. The report continued by claiming that the North American swine flu seems to be on an "evolutionary fast track," with changes in "animal husbandry" spurring the rapid shift. One of these changes is growth in the "percentage of farms with 5,000 or more animals," which "surged from 18% in 1993 to 53% in 2002."[22]

As production intensifies and consolidates into the hands of fewer producers, rural America's economic health suffers as well. Poverty in rural areas rises. A study conducted by the faculty of the School of Public Health at the University of North Carolina concluded that the locations of "approximately 2,500 intensive hog confinement facilities" fell "disproportionately in communities with higher levels of poverty."[23] As North Carolina moved from "fifteenth to second in hog production among U.S. states" between 1985 and 1998, the number of hogs outnumbered humans—10 million hogs compared to approximately 7.5 million humans.[24] The same study determined that "there is a net decrease in jobs in regions where hog production has been industrialized because of the displacement of the independent producers who purchased locally."[25]

Furthermore, if those issues were not reason enough to show that CAFOs are highly problematic, according to a 2006 United Nations report, greenhouse gas emissions from *livestock operations* account for 18 percent of all human-caused greenhouse gas emissions, exceeding emissions from transportation. Yes, you read that correctly, even more than what one drives, what one eats impacts Earth's climate.[26]

With the other negative consequences of CAFOs now noted, I turn to what they mean for animal welfare or, more accurately, the absence thereof. I will warn you, even a brief glimpse into animal welfare issues in the CAFO system can be completely overwhelming. As the aforementioned report clearly states, it is "an ethical dilemma that transcends objective scientific measure."[27] Pigs, chickens, cows, turkeys, and sheep who end up in intensive factory farming operations live lives that are short, painful, and unhealthy. Below are a few specific examples, but in general all of these animals are confined to extremely small spaces, are filled with antibiotics because of the toxic conditions, and die in painful, traumatic ways.

Smithfield Foods is the nation's largest pig producer. In order to slaughter over 400,000 pigs each day in the U.S., Smithfield Foods must reproduce the pigs quickly and maximize space. The result: "a bedlam of squealing, chain rattling, and horrible roaring." As Matthew Scully describes of his experience in a Smithfield mass confinement farm in North Carolina,

> [t]o maximize the use of space and minimize the need for care, the creatures are encased row after row, 400- to 500-pound mammals trapped without relief inside iron crates 7 feet long and 22 inches wide. They chew maniacally on bars and chains, as foraging animals will do when denied straw, or engage in stereotypical nest building with straw that isn't there, or else just lie there like broken beings . . . The smallest scraps of human charity—a bit of maternal care, room to roam outdoors, straw to lie on—have long since been taken away as costly luxuries, and so the pigs know

the feel only of concrete and metal. They lie covered in their own urine and excrement, with broken legs from trying to escape or just to turn, covered with festering sores, tumors, ulcers, lesions, or what my guide shrugged off as the routine "pus pockets."[28]

The image of the farm that many of us recognize in the movie *Babe* is from a time and a place that no longer exists in industrialized American agriculture. The beginning of that movie, though, gives a hint of the current system. In these operations, some female infants are kept for future breeding. The rest of the piglets, however, endure this fate: they have their tails cut off with pliers, they have their teeth pulled, and they are confined in extremely tight quarters for five or six months until they are shipped to slaughter plants. Pigs are intelligent creatures who exhibit strong emotional connections to each other. Yet in our system they never root in the dirt or wallow in a pond, and they never even breathe clean air in their short, painful lives.

Not all of the animals on these large CAFOs are bred for their meat. Dairy cattle, for example, are obviously used for mass production of milk. Since mammals produce milk to feed newborn offspring, a cow must be impregnated frequently in order to keep her milk production high. Because she needs to produce milk constantly to serve the dairy industry, mastitis (an inflammation of the udder) occurs frequently. In 2007, over 85 percent of dairy operations in the U.S. reported treating cows with antibiotics for mastitis.[29] Combined with the fact that her milk production decreases significantly after she turns three, the stress of constant pregnancies leads to a shortened life span for a dairy cow. While the natural life span for a cow is approximately twenty years, dairy cattle are usually slaughtered when they are about five years old. Often at this point they are "too weak to walk or even stand" and are "herded onto trucks and sent quickly to the nearest slaughterhouse."[30] These cows are usually referred to as "downers," since they are unable to move themselves. A recent report by the HSUS revealed the conditions under which they are transported to slaughter. In their investigation, "workers are seen kicking cows, ramming them with the blades of a forklift, jabbing them in the eyes, applying painful electrical shocks and even torturing them with a hose and water in attempts to force sick or injured animals to walk to slaughter."[31] On its website, the HSUS provides visual documentary evidence of the downed cows as well. While slaughtering downed cows and introducing them into the food system is technically illegal, it still takes place. Those dairy cattle who make it through their years in the milk production system, even if they are still able to walk, are slaughtered for ground meat.

Though I will not address it in depth at this point, a side product of the dairy industry is veal. Veal, the meat from a baby cow, results from the number of times that cows must be impregnated. Suffice it to say that veal calves live short lives in small crates that prevent them from developing any muscle mass. They are forcibly taken from their mothers before they can nurse, since the milk is required for the dairy industry. Veal production is among the most violent and least humane of all forms of meat systems in the world.

There are numerous resources available to help people learn more about the suffering of animals in the food production system in the U.S.; many of these are listed at the back of the book. It is also important to keep in mind that the system, unfortunately perfected in the U.S., is now being exported to other parts of the world as well. Factory farming is on the rise in India and China as the populations of those two countries increase dramatically the meat in their diets. It is becoming a global problem of cruelty and environmental degradation.

With these stark and difficult images in mind, I turn to some ideas about how Christianity might address CAFOs. It is not difficult to do, even though it seems that contemporary Christianity has rarely, if ever, thought about it much. Why Christians have not considered the welfare of animals in the food production system is in itself a troubling question that I will touch on in the final chapter. For now, however, it is most constructive to ask how Christians might respond.

Eating Mercifully

In the summer of 2008 I was lucky enough to take part in the production of the documentary *Eating Mercifully*. The idea behind this piece and an entire campaign by the HSUS is to remind religious practitioners that food and religion are not separate from each other. What we eat reflects what we believe. The basic premise behind *Eating Mercifully* is that Christianity has as a central tenet the idea of compassion and that compassion is not exclusively limited to relationships between and among humans.[32]

Eating Mercifully does show some scenes of the horrors of factory farming. Chickens are distraught in battery cages as they pick the feathers from each other; while they are still alive and in pain, downer cows are moved with fork-lifts through a meatpacking facility; pigs are shown living in tiny crates, chewing at the bars to try to get free. But the scenes are actually relatively mild compared to what happens in many CAFO settings. During filming the producer told me that they carefully chose images that would convey the brutality, but that they chose not to include the most horrific scenes because people would not be able to watch. How has our food production system evolved to a point that it would horrify us to see it?

Rooterville Sanctuary pigs being fed by Elaine West,
the founder of the sanctuary.

While I was invited to share ideas from the history of Christianity that might provide insight on factory farming, Elaine West described her commitment to rescuing animals from factory farms. Along with her partner Dale, she established and runs Rooterville, A Sanctuary Inc., a place in Florida where animals once destined to enter the violence of the factory farming industry live out their lives in peace.[33] The Wests, who are evangelical and committed Christians, find their calling to run the sanctuary deep in their religious belief system. And they are not the only ones.

A brief overview of the history of food in Christianity points to the link between eating and religious beliefs and practices. But what about eating animals, specifically animals who come from an industrial factory farming system? While it cannot be claimed that Christianity offers a clear answer to this question, some responses do resonate much more powerfully than others.

Numerous secular scholars have argued that Christianity is inherently speciesist, that in Christian thinking humans are the only ones who matter to God. Lynn White Jr. did so in his classic 1967 essay "The Historical Roots of our Ecological Crisis" and Peter Singer makes a similar case in his seminal book *Animal Liberation*. They, among others, suggest that such concepts as the dominion of humans over the world, as expressed in the book of Genesis, and the incarnation of God as a human make Christianity irredeemable from the perspective of animal concerns. In their eyes, in the Christian tradition other animals simply do not and cannot matter.

But much evidence suggests otherwise. Yes, I will admit that it is difficult to find an abundance of evidence to suggest that all Christians should, for example, be vegetarians. However, there is within Christianity's great history and tradition a significant, concrete foundation for a compassionate approach to all animals, even those that might become food. A number of excellent essays address the call to compassion in biblical texts, but I will re-emphasize a few of the particularly pertinent passages here.[34]

Examples of compassion to and consideration of animals abound in the Hebrew Bible (Old Testament). Rebecca, for instance, is selected to be the wife of Isaac because she offered water to a stranger's camel (Genesis 24). In Numbers 22, Balaam is rebuked for his cruelty to his ass, the animal who saved him from the angel of death. God reminds Job that animals are part of God's creation and that Job is not the center of everything (Job 39). The Psalms point to God's compassion: "giving drink to every wild animal" and causing "the grass to grow for the cattle" (Psalm 104). And the preacher in Ecclesiastes points to the similarities between animals and humans: "For the fate of humans and the fate of animals is the same; as one dies, so dies the other. They all have the same breath, and humans have no advantage over the animals . . ." (Ecclesiastes 3).

Though in comparison the New Testament canon has few references to animals, the references it contains are both telling and instructive. In Mark 1, Jesus spends time alone with the wild animals, and interestingly, this is one of the times when he is fasting and in prayer. Other passages that are noticed more often include Jesus' reference to the value of the sparrows to God, and Paul's insistence in the Letter to the Romans that the entire creation groans for salvation: "the creation itself will be set free from its bondage to decay and will obtain the freedom of the glory of the children of God (Romans 8:21). Extracanonical works include even more accounts of both Jesus and some of his other early followers engaged with animals. For the purposes of this chapter, it seems that the most important extracanonical work is the story of the encounter between Jesus, his disciples, and the injured pack animal, found in a Coptic apocryphal work:

> There they found a man with a sumpter-mule. But the animal had fallen for the burden was too heavy, and he beat it that it bled. And Jesus came to him and said, Man why dost thou beat thine animal? Seest thou not that it is too weak for its burden, and knowest thou not that it suffers pains? But the man answered and said, What is that to you? I can beat it as much as I please, since it is my property, and I bought it for a good sum of money . . . But the Lord said, Do you notice how it bleeds, and hear you not how it laments and cries? But they answered and said, Nay Lord, we hear not how it laments and cries. And the Lord was sad and exclaimed, Woe to you, that ye hear not how it complains to the Creator in heaven, and cries for mercy.

But three times woe to him of whom it complains and cries in its distress. And he came forth and touched the animal. And it arose and its wounds were healed. And Jesus said to the man, Now go on and beat it no more, that you also may find mercy.[35]

Even though its origin is unknown, this powerful account of Jesus' compassion and of God's care for all animals rings true to orthodox Christian belief. It is reminiscent of Jesus' commandment to break the Sabbath in order to save an animal who fell into a ditch—"If one of you has a child or an ox that has fallen into a well, will you not immediately pull it out on a Sabbath day?" (Luke 14)—and of Jesus' recognition that dogs do deserve to eat (Luke 7:24-30).

But even more directly, the overarching theme of compassion for the "least," the ones who have no voice of their own, is a central Christian doctrine. Those who are last will be first in the world described by Jesus. Thus, a system that necessarily inflicts long-term pain and removes creatures from any semblance of the conditions under which they would naturally live does not fall under the umbrella of compassion and mercy.

Matthew Scully in his book *Dominion* suggests that Christians must rethink how to enact "dominion." He contends that humans are indeed placed by God in a position of power over the creation. Dominion should, he argues, be exercised with care and compassion—a valid theological approach to the issue of factory farming. Even if humans do have dominion, it must be exercised with care for all other creatures.

From the history and theology of Christianity, however, I think the position is even stronger than that of benevolent dominion. Rather, I have found there is a call for active compassion in all that we do. And what is more central to what we do than eating? In order to show mercy, Christians should consider refusing to participate in a system that perpetuates pain and suffering on a scale that is unfathomable. When tens of billions of animals suffer cruel deaths annually, and only after living painful and distressed lives, it is an imperative for Christians, at the least, to refuse to participate in the system.

So what are the alternatives? How can one realistically refuse to participate in such a pervasive system? We can practice a compassionate vegetarianism, at least on a small scale at first if the task seems daunting. Selecting one day a week to eliminate animal products would be congruent with the many generations of Christians who abstained from these products on Fridays in solidarity with the crucified Jesus. Holding compassionate potlucks, and using these events to educate the congregation and larger community, creates a new possibility for agape meals or love feasts. Finding local, humane products to replace mass-produced, unhealthy, and cruel products is another component of a merciful eating lifestyle. Participating in a blessing of food animals in conjunction with the Feast of Saint Francis opens the world of the farm animal to the rituals of the church. All of these are steps in the direction of a truly compassionate Christian life.

A number of Christian communities and individuals are already moving in this direction. The example of Rooterville Sanctuary is just one of many. Not only do a variety of major denominations have official statements regarding animals and food, but local congregations are beginning to take part in these discussions and actions. According to Christine Gutleben, director of the HSUS' Animals and Religion program, by October of 2008 thousands had signed the All Creatures Great and Small pledge.[36] The pledge, outlined on the HSUS website states that eating is a moral activity with spiritual significance and points to the connections between food and faith in religious traditions. It also points to the official statements on animal welfare of U.S. religious communities.

In the book *The Face on Your Plate*, mentioned above, Jeffrey Masson considers the question of animal happiness. Some animal behaviorists, he points out, claim that we can never know what makes an animal happy, but he argues differently, pointing to what to most is really quite obvious:

> Animals are happy if they can live in conformity with their own nature, using to the utmost those traits in a natural setting. To live according to nature will differ for each species, but the answers are unfathomable mysteries. Cows are herd animals. When transported in dark trains to the slaughterhouse, they cannot help but feel panic. You cannot speak of happiness inside that boxcar. Cows did not evolve to take such terminal voyages. Nor did cows ever have to face a situation where their newborn calves were removed from them at birth. The calling sound they make is a mourning call; it cannot be mistaken for a happy sound.

He continues to provide a list of the clear, basic necessities for geese (who are monogamous, more so than humans), ducks (who need water, not indoor pens), chickens (who love to take a sunbath), and sheep (who need a leader among them).[37]

Still, an astonishing 80 percent of Americans think that animals lead happy lives before they become meat.[38] As a society we are so many steps removed from the animals when they are alive and when they are in the various stages of the industrial meat production system, that most of us are totally unaware of the process. As people of faith, Christians are called to take on the responsibility of raising awareness and shedding light on the dark sheds that hide the suffering of animals from view.

To close this chapter, I again borrow an insightful theological observation by Masson. If God is the Creator, through whatever process one might believe (*ex nihilo*, evolution, etc.), then certainly the way animals were created to live is the way that they should be able to live. Humans have, at this juncture in history, so skewed that natural order just to fill a ravenous appetite for a meat-heavy diet (a diet that is not even a healthy one for us), that both humans and animals are suffering. Animals suffer unspeakable misery. Certainly, just as God heard the cry of the injured mule, God hears the cries of the suffering cows, pigs, and chickens in our factory farms. And, according to the response of Jesus to the suffering of the animal, God reacts with compassion and *calls on us humans to do so as well.*

Chapter 4

===========================

Good Christian Hospitality
Animals at Home on the Earth

For endangered species we are both their greatest enemy
and their only hope.
Those wonderful creatures will not argue their case.
They will not put up a fight.
They will not beg for reprieve.
They will not say goodbye.
They will not cry out.
They will just vanish.
And after they are gone, there will be silence.
And there will be stillness.
And there will be empty places . . .
With so many lives hanging in the balance,
the paths we choose today will decide the fate
of the world.[1]

Today we human beings are only beginning to recognize our power over the earth. And, tragically, in the interim, thousands of other species are disappearing from the earth forever. Most scientists contend the earth may be entering a great period of mass extinction, and unless we act soon—and dramatically—majestic animals like the blue whale, the polar bear, and far too many others who are less frequently noticed may be gone. What are the reasons for this extinction? Almost all of these scientists agree that it is caused, among other things, by anthropogenic factors. Simply said, we are causing the deaths of numerous other species by the ways we are living on this planet.[2]

What does this mean for Christianity? Does it matter that by the year 2025 all tigers will be extinct in the wild? Should it concern Christians that the passenger pigeon will never be seen again and that the inheritance of this bird is gone forever? What, in this day, should we humans think of the biblical injunction to "be fruitful and multiply"? Did God really desire for humans to take up all the space on the planet at the cost of tens of thousands of other species? In this chapter, we will explore these questions from a particular and compelling perspective: the perspective of Christian hospitality.

At its core, Christianity is a religion of hospitality. But what does that really mean? In her study of Christian hospitality, Christine Pohl, professor of church in society at Asbury Seminary, claims, "Hospitality to the least, without expectation of benefit of repayment, remained the normative commitment by which each generation measured its practice."[3] From the biblical texts, where Jesus instructs his disciples to go out and seek the homes that would welcome them; to the medieval period, when wandering monks lived day-to-day based on the generosity of others; to the contemporary world, where many open their doors to house the homeless when local shelters are bursting at the seams, hospitality is a core principle at the heart of Christianity.[4]

Is there a way to apply this principle to the planet? To be welcoming to those with whom we share the creation? When considering these questions, I suspect most of us will immediately think of ourselves as the hosts rather than the guests; the host is the one in control of the situation. Yet the earth does not belong to human beings. It is not a home that we own. Even the most traditional of Christian interpretations of life acknowledges that the creation belongs to the Creator, not to humans. It is God who offers hospitality, even to humans. In the Scriptures and the theological history of Christianity, it is clear: the earth is neither ours to give nor ours to take away.

Nevertheless, we humans have lived out the concept of "dominion" to such an extreme that we now inhabit almost every corner of the planet. Our use of space and of resources assumes that humans possess the authority of ownership. This is *our* home, first and foremost, and other animals (and plants) live or die at our discretion, under our control. I know this seems like a harsh pronouncement. But when one steps outside oneself to think as objectively as possible, it is difficult to conceive of the current state of the earth and of human impact on it in any other way. As I write, the United Nations Climate Change Conference is in full swing. Delegates are debating the impact of humans on the earth's climate. People dressed in polar bear suits wear shirts that proclaim "Save Humans Too." Economically developing countries challenge the wealthier countries to help finance clean energy all over the planet. And, in the meantime, animal habitats are being lost daily while other animals have no homes left.

Why, then, does hospitality leap out to me as a way for Christians to ponder species extinction and human responses to it? Undeniably there are times in the history of the tradition when Christians have not lived up to the ideal of hospitality. Indeed, Christians took the lead in a number of horrible and tragic events as inquisitors, as conquistadors, as slave owners, and even as popes and missionaries, some of whom were anything but hospitable to humans, not to mention other animals. In the twenty-first century the openness of various congregations and denominations to all humans is still fiercely debated. Hospitality proves a difficult goal, and when we do not realize it, it can, literally, be deadly. Despite our moments of shortcoming throughout our history, there is strong evidence that hospitality is central to the tradition and needs to be considered thoughtfully, continually, and seriously; it cannot be negated. As beloved priest and author Henri Nouwen stated so eloquently, "If there is any concept worth restoring to its original depth and evocative potential, it is the concept of hospitality."[5]

To examine several twenty-first-century issues related to hospitality and other species, we will look first at just a few of the biblical calls to hospitality and the development of this ideal in the history of the tradition. Paramount issues are destruction of or invasion of habitat that exacerbate the tenuous position of endangered species (and continue to drive species to extinction) and the need to create or designate spaces for wildlife to live abundantly. While almost all of the topics in this book could, arguably, come under the umbrella of hospitality (sharing our homes with pets, rethinking the way we treat food animals), I here focus particularly on place and shared space on Earth. The vast number of resources is truly overwhelming, which speaks volumes to the centrality of hospitality in Christianity.

Hospitality as Sacred Duty

Early in the Hebrew Bible, Sarah and Abraham, often seen as the "parents" of the Israelites, set the standard for hospitality when in Genesis 18 three strangers wander past their home. Abraham enthusiastically runs out to greet them, invites them in for food and rest, and prepares a marvelous feast—all for these three people who are strangers to his household. As the story tells, Abraham's hospitality does not go unnoticed or unrewarded by God. As many will recall, God grants Sarah and Abraham a miracle: Sarah becomes pregnant in her old age, bearing the child for whom she has longed her entire life. From this might we infer that hospitality, therefore, is a two-way street? When hospitality is offered freely and graciously, the host gains as much as the stranger who is welcomed. A pattern is thus established that is repeated throughout the Hebrew Bible, New Testament, and stories of saints in the history of Christianity: strangers who need a place to rest often turn out to be divine visitors; the truly faithful provide hospitality with grace and abundance. There are myriad reasons to offer hospitality, and God seems to constantly stress the significance of hospitable acts.[6]

But in the biblical texts hospitality is only extended to other humans, right? Actually, no, not at all. Consider Genesis 24, which recounts the story of Rebekah and some of Abraham's camels. When Rebekah finds one of Abraham's servants and ten camels resting at a well, she offers them water, including the thirsty animals, and attends to the various needs of *both* the human *and* the camels. Later in Genesis, a story about Jacob and Rachel, another generation in the genealogy of the Israelites, emphasizes that the communal well is a place of hospitality for the sheep who gather as well as for the humans.

> As [Jacob] looked, he saw a well in the field and three flocks of sheep lying there beside it; for out of that well the flocks were watered. The stone on the well's mouth was large, and when all the flocks were gathered there, the shepherds would roll the stone from the mouth of the well, and water the sheep.[7] (Genesis 29:1-3)

These watering holes are provided for all of God's creatures to share in common.[8]

Further into the canon, one will find additional evidence that the earth is a home for all creatures and that God's gift of resources is for all of life. Perhaps the most powerful pronouncement is found in Psalm 104. Originally written as a song or other piece of worship material, Psalm 104 proclaims that God makes springs that give "drink to every wild animal," and next to these streams the "birds of the air have their habitation." Places are designated just for other animals to inhabit as their homes.. In the fir trees "the stork has its home," and the high mountains are "for the wild goats." It is from God that the lions receive their food, and, because God placed them there, the sea is full of innumerable creeping things. Praise for divine hospitality and for the centrality of animals to the whole picture of life on Earth is central to the vision of this psalm.[9]

I do not intend to oversimplify or glorify these stories of hospitality. According to the Psalm, God's hospitality does indeed extend to all of Earth's inhabitants. But even the exemplars of human hospitality fall short, as is evident in the continuing saga of Abraham and Sarah. Though they did welcome the three strangers, as many will recall, they later expelled Hagar (Sarah's servant) and Ishmael (her son with Abraham) from their home. In biblical times, as it is today, hospitality was an ideal that was difficult to achieve.[10]

The ancient Mediterranean culture, the setting in which Christianity was born, itself placed much emphasis on hospitality. Without question, Mediterranean codes of expected conduct had significant influence on early Christianity, but Christianity changed these ideas of hospitality dramatically. In the larger ancient Mediterranean culture, hospitality was largely construed to mean reciprocity between the host and the guest. This was particularly true in the traditions of that area impacted by Hellenistic (Greek) cultural norms. And in this Hellenistic culture, the guests were usually influential members of the community; they were often among the more powerful people able to return the favors bestowed to them.[11] For example, historians believe that upon arriving into a village travelers would gather at a communal well (reminiscent of the passages in Genesis 24 and 29) and wait for an offer of hospitality from a usually prosperous local resident.[12] Once hospitality was extended, the host assumed responsibility for the guest's overall well-being. In return the guests bore gifts to the host or offered to extend hospitality to them in the future. In the earliest Christian practices, however, the expectation of reciprocity was dropped; followers were required to be hospitable *without receiving anything in return*. Canonical Gospel texts provide a clue into the reasoning behind the change.

Matthew 25 and Luke 14 are foundational texts for this radical notion of hospitality that expanded the boundaries for early Christianity. The passage in Matthew depicts Jesus as the judge who separates the "sheep" from the "goats":

> When the Son of Man comes in his glory . . . he will separate people one from another as a shepherd separates the sheep from the goats, and he will put the sheep at his right hand and the goats at the left . . . "Come, you that are blessed by my Father, inherit the kingdom prepared for you from the foundation of the world; for I was hungry and you gave me food, I was thirsty and you gave me something to drink, I was a stranger and you welcomed me, I was naked and you gave me clothing, I was sick and you took care of me, I was in prison and you visited me." (Matthew 25:31-46)

Those who are saved welcomed the stranger, among other acts of hospitality; those who are condemned did not. The Scripture continues with a parallel for those who did not welcome the stranger. They are "accursed" and "sent away into eternal punishment" for not offering the welcome. This judgment scene parallels the growing hospitality culture for Christians. The people who offer hospitality (the host) receive a gift from the guest; in this case the guest in the Matthew passage is Jesus, and the gift is salvation and the honored seat at the right hand of God. Those who do not offer hospitality do not receive that gift.

It is also extremely significant that the stranger in this passage is identified with those who are naked, sick, and imprisoned. In other words, the stranger seeking refuge is no longer the influential person, but the least of these. That dramatic shift in roles points to a radical change in the concept of hospitality for early Christianity.

Another passage in the Gospel of Luke directly confronts notions of hospitality. Here Jesus tells the parable of the great feast. He says,

> When you give a luncheon or a dinner, do not invite your friends or your brothers or your relatives or your rich neighbors, in case they may invite you in return, and you would be repaid. But when you give a banquet, invite the poor, the crippled, the lame, and the blind. And you will be blessed, because they cannot repay you, for you will be repaid at the resurrection of the righteous. (Luke 14:12-14)

Inviting the poor, the lame, and the crippled into your home and to your table was a truly revolutionary act in ancient Mediterranean purity cultures. Rigid "purity" rules identified for each group or class of people with whom one was allowed to eat; in so doing, these rules also identified those who could not eat together. As stories spread of Jesus' willingness to break these purity rules and to dine with anyone, the notion of extending hospitality continued to expand as well, culminating in the practice of open table fellowship, a central concept in early Christianity.[13]

New Testament scholar John Dominic Crossan calls this tent of early Christianity "open commensality"—or, in other words, opening the table of fellowship to anyone; while it focuses in particular on the social context of the shared meal, its foundational meaning is much broader and encompasses a new sense of radical egalitarianism. As Crossan rightly explains, the "open commensality and radical egalitarianism of Jesus' Kingdom of God are more terrifying than anything we have ever imagined."[14] Does this radical vision limit itself to human beings alone? While that might have been the gist of the meaning in some of the parables and actions of Jesus as recounted in the early texts, there are also passages that point to an all-encompassing reach. From Matthew 6:26 ("Look at the birds of the air; they neither sow nor reap nor gather into barns, and yet your heavenly Father feeds them.") to Mark 7:28 (". . . even the dogs under the table eat the children's crumbs"), there is ample evidence of an underlying assumption: that God opens the table to all creatures.

There are numerous other examples of hospitality in the canonical texts and even more in the extracanonical writings from early Christianity.[15] Because of this early foundation, by the fourth century, when Christianity was established as a legal religion, the framework of hospitality was essential. Early preachers, historians, and saints all focus on the foundational nature of hospitality for all Christians.[16] For example, Commodianus, a third-century Christian poet, writes, "Those of you who seek to feed the other, and have prepared what you could by assiduously feeding, have done the right thing."[17] And John Chrysostom, the fourth-century preacher and bishop of Constantinople who left the myriad sermons that provide great insight into the early church, pronounced, "Observe, the hospitality here spoken of is not merely a friendly reception, but one given with zeal and full of life, with readiness, and going about it as if one were receiving Christ Himself."[18]

It is with this foundation of radical hospitality in mind that Saint Jerome (ca. 342–420), an early monastic leader and one of the first four "doctors" or major intellectual leaders of the church, emphasized the practice for his community.

> Our duties in our monastery are those of hospitality. We welcome all who come to us with the smile of human friendliness. We must take care lest it should again happen that Mary and Joseph do not find room in the inn, and that Jesus should be shut out. . . .[19]

This commanding pronouncement provides a fitting bridge to our next section, in which our attention turns pointedly to animals in the history of Christian hospitality. Do you know of Jerome's most famous guest? Of his iconographic symbol for the last sixteen centuries? He was a lion.

Animals and Hospitality in the Lives of Saints

The Golden Legend, a thirteenth-century collection of stories of the lives of saints that was very influential in medieval Europe, retells this account of Saint Jerome and the lion.[20]

> One day toward evening, when he was seated with the brethren to hear the sacred lessons read, a lion suddenly limped into the monastery. The other monks fled at the sight of the beast, but Jerome greeted him as a guest. The lion showed him his wounded foot, and Jerome called the brothers and ordered them to wash the animal's feet and to dress the wound carefully. When they set about doing this, they found that the paw had been scratched and torn by thorns. They did what was necessary, and the lion recovered, lost all his wildness, and lived among the monks like a house pet.[21]

As the rest of his biography goes, Jerome and the lion became great companions, so much so that the lion died from grief shortly after Jerome's passing. So it is one of the very first intellectual and spiritual leaders of the church, Saint Jerome, who is even now most often pictured with this animal companion. While the majority of animals never will and never should be domesticated, a basic requirement it would seem for animals to be pets or companions, this story of one of the most beloved saints shows the extent of the Christian call to hospitality and the role of the saints in exemplifying it.

In the many stories of the Christian saints, it is often those of desert dwellers or wilderness ascetics that reveal a close, even spiritual, relationship with animals. And these stories were well-known by Christians during the Middle Ages. From the stories, the Christians of that time learned lessons about how to live, they celebrated the saints' feast days each year—celebrations that were often accompanied by the oral recitation of the stories of the saints' lives—and they believed that these saints would help them attain salvation. As we saw in chapter 3, Paul the Hermit, often considered the first of the wilderness ascetics, was fed each day by a raven. Upon her death, Saint Mary of Egypt, who lived from about 344 to 421 C.E., the last of those years as a hermit in the desert, was buried by a friendly lion.[22] As we hear from the Desert Fathers and Mothers, whose stories and sayings were recorded and became central devotional texts for Eastern Orthodox Christians, God provided Abba Macarius with an antelope to fend off his starvation. But here is an important twist: he did not eat her; rather, she allowed him to nurse.[23] And Simeon Stylites, one of the most important Syrian saints, who lived most of his life on top of a tall pillar, defended a pregnant hind (a young deer) from men who wanted to kill and eat her.[24] I could go on and on. The tradition is so rich with these stories. Truly, the legends of the saints and their animals are legion.[25] You can learn more of them in the Additional Resources listed in the back of this book. But in the rest of our space here, I would like to focus on two saints in particular: Sulpicius Severus and Saint Brigit of Kildare.

The life of Sulpicius Severus (ca. 360–420), a historian and well-known holy man most often remembered for his biography of Saint Martin of Tours, seems to directly connect hospitality and animals. Severus was an anchorite, one who chooses to seclude him or herself by being walled up in a small room connected to a church or by leaving for the wilderness, in order to detach from the temptations of the world. But Severus chose not to remove himself from relationships with animals. He opened his desert cell to them and shared miraculous healing powers with them. A wolf, for example, was "accustomed to stand near him at dinner" and "waited at the door until [Severus] offered her the bread leftover from his own humble dinner." Unfortunately, when Severus was away from his cell she decided to help herself. And then she felt exceedingly guilty about it. When Severus returned and discovered the bread was missing, he did not become angry but instead was "deeply grieved," disheartened that she was not there for their regular shared meal. Severus' prayers to God, however, brought her back. She approached timidly with her "eyes cast upon the earth from profound shame" and seemed to "beg, in a sort of way, for pardon." Severus felt pity for her, stroked her head and gave her "two loaves instead of one," thus reconciling the two so they could resume their friendship.

In another recorded incident, Severus took his hospitality on the road. While on a journey with several friends, "they beheld a lioness of remarkable size coming towards them." She immediately approached Severus and lay at his feet weeping. Severus knew she wanted him to follow her, so he did. Eventually they arrived at her den where he found her five newly born cubs. The cubs were blind, having "come forth with closed eyes from the womb." One by one she brought them out and "laid them down at the feet of the anchorite." And what did he do? Severus called on God to heal them. He touched their closed eyes and in so doing restored their sight.[26]

The hagiographical accounts of Saint Brigit of Kildare, a fifth-century Celtic Christian, also tell a wide range of stories about her life with animals. Celtic Christianity developed in some areas of England, Scotland, Wales, and Ireland as well as in the far western areas of France. This particular form of Christianity developed somewhat apart from the influences of the Mediterranean ethos. Still today remnants of a number of fascinating pre-Christian traditions are evident in this unique form of Christianity's rituals, stories, and patterns. Saint Patrick is, of course, among the most well-known of the Celtic saints, as his story and feast day moved into U.S. culture with Irish immigrants. (And the rest, as they say, is history.) But Saint Brigit is, in many ways, as important as Patrick to the history of Celtic Christianity.

And Saint Brigit's hospitality to animals was given in many forms. As but one example, when a wild boar was being hunted and came "running out of the woods in terror and suddenly landed in the midst of blessed Brigit's pigs," she neither scared him off nor revealed him to the hunters. Rather, Brigit "noted its arrival and pronounced a blessing upon it." And so it happened that the wild boar settled down and safely hid among the domestic herd, escaping imminent death at the hands of the hunters.[27]

In another account of Saint Brigit's life, Dubthach, her father, asks her to cook a piece of bacon for their guest. This

standard hospitality for an influential traveler is subverted
when a hungry dog approaches Brigit. Recognizing the dog's
hunger, the saint gives him "one-fifth of the bacon," and
when the dog still appears hungry she gives him another
fifth. Yet, when Brigit's father returns and counts the pieces
of bacon, he finds them all there. None were missing. The
human guest, who witnessed the whole incident, tells Brigit's
father about the dog. After this, "a portion of the food was
distributed among the poor." In response to the entire incident, Dubthach later exclaimed that his daughter performed
many miracles, suggesting that feeding the dog was the precursor to the rest. In this story the dog seems to represent
the divine guest in disguise, and, as usual, because of Brigit's
hospitality, God granted a miracle.[28]

All of these wonderful stories of saints with animals
speak loudly to the radical extension of Christian hospitality
to all animals. Francis of Assisi, Aventine of Troyes, Kieran
of Ireland, Clare of Assisi, and Martín of Porres are just a
few more saints whose lives and stories add manifold more
evidence and examples. Each of these holy people was closely
connected to animals and sought after their well-being; they
extended hospitality to the entire creation.

Also, as these stories attest, though it has often gone
unnoticed in the history of Christianity, humans are not the
only ones who offer hospitality. Other animals do so as well,
providing safety, food, and companionship to humans. Stories like these abound in the tradition. The most popular of
stories are accounts of the nativity, depicted in the artwork
of the church for centuries, and include the adoring ox and
ass who share their home with the baby Jesus. While these
two pivotal characters are not present in the canonical Gospels, by the sixth century they appear in devotional images,
maybe originally in the Sancta Sanctorum icon, an incredibly

significant piece of art that gives us insight into popular religious practices in early Christianity.[29] Here, and in countless images that follow, the ox and the ass nuzzle up against the divine child, providing him comfort and warmth. The apocryphal work *The Gospel of Pseudo-Matthew*, probably written in the ninth century, is, as far as we know, the first text that actually mentions these two welcoming animals. In this gospel, Mary gives birth to Jesus in a cave and then, on the third day, leaves and enters a stable; she places the child in the manger, "and an ox and an ass adored him."[30] Though most do not know of it by name, this text has had a great influence on medieval art and iconography, as well as on present-day conceptions of the nativity.

But the images in popular art and the story in that gospel are just the beginning of the stories about the infant Jesus, animals, and hospitality. Later, *The Gospel of Pseudo-Matthew* gives an account of the holy family heading into the desert. Since this was the home for wild animals, "lions and panthers adored [the baby Jesus] and accompanied them." These desert dwellers "went before them showing them the way and bowing their heads." Not only did the animals escort the holy family through the wilderness, but the great carnivores that came upon them left in peace the animals accompanying Jesus:

> . . . the lions kept walking with them, and with the oxen and the asses and the beasts of burden which carried what they needed, and did not hurt a single one of them, though they remained with them; they were tame among the sheep and the rams which they had brought with them from Judaea and which they had with them. They walked among wolves and feared nothing; and not one of them was hurt by another . . . There were two oxen and a waggon [*sic*] in which they carried their necessities, and the lions directed them in their path.[31]

This wilderness was a place of danger, and it was made safe for Jesus, Mary, and Joseph by the very animals who would otherwise have been threatening. Not only did they prevent harm, but the animals guided the holy family to safety, literally walking the family peacefully through their own territory. The animals welcomed the infant into their homes, first into the manger and then into the desert, and provided companionship, rest, and safe passage. Hospitality *par excellence.*

Striking accounts of animal hospitality also come from Celtic Christianity and the early Irish saints. Take, for example, the wonderful "Voyage of Brendan," which recounts the journeys of the saint and his companions as they traveled from island to island around the northern seas. The entire account is full of lessons in hospitality, since the brothers relied on being welcomed and given provisions each time they landed. At one point Saint Brendan and his companions arrived on a "rocky and bare" island where they "passed the night in the open in prayer." The next morning they began to unload fish from the boat, built a fire, and put a pot on the wood to cook the fish. Suddenly, when the pot began to boil, "the island started to heave like a wave." The brothers fled to the boat, and, when all were safely aboard, "the island began to move across the surface of the sea." Brendan then explained to them that they did not need to be afraid, God had told him that the island was "nothing other than a sea animal, the foremost of all that swim in the oceans," and his name was Jasconius.[32] Yes, the sojourning holy men had spent the night peacefully on the back of a whale—a whale whom the saint, and by implication God, knew by name.

Later in their journey, Brendan and his companions meet a hermit, one fittingly also named Paul. Reminiscent of the other Paul the Hermit mentioned above, this Paul lived off the generosity of an animal for decades. And who was his companion? A sea otter. When Paul first arrived at his isolated island home, a sea otter would come to him straight from the sea "walking on its hind legs, carrying a fish in its jaws and with a bundle of twigs for making a fire between its front legs." For thirty years this otter provided for Paul, bringing him his fish every third day.[33]

Yes, in the lives of the saints, the stories of encounters between animals and humans are striking and abundant. Humans and animals offer each other the gift of hospitality, usually without expecting anything in return. It is a model that exemplifies the radical notion that developed early in the tradition and carried through the Middle Ages. Isn't it sad that so many Christians today have never heard the stories of their lives? While there are instances of radical hospitality in the more recent history of Christianity, unfortunately animals are not included in the circle nearly as frequently. Why? There are a variety of complicated historical reasons, including the rise of humanism and the shift of various technological systems. As humans became and continue to become more urban and less connected to animals and the natural world around them, animals are increasingly removed from the sacred circle of hospitality. Sadly, at the dawn of the twenty-first century, when many animals face extinction at our hands, these stories are rarely told in the churches and Sunday schools in the Christian world. Yet at no other time has the question of welcoming, including, and making space for animals been so vitally important.

Species Extinction

*Love the animals: God gave them the rudiments of
thought and an untroubled joy. Do not trouble it, do not
torment them, do not take their joy from them, do not go
against God's purpose. Man, do not exalt yourself above
the animals: they are sinless, and you, you with your gran-
deur, fester the earth by your appearance on it, and leave
your festering trace behind you—alas, almost every one of
us does!*

—Fyodor Dostoevsky[34]

In his sermon quoted above, Father Zosima, the spiritual
center in Fyodor Dostoevsky's acclaimed and deeply theological novel, implores us to humbly love animals rather than
destroy them. He acknowledges as well that humans "fester" the earth, an interesting way to describe our impact.
Though written in the late nineteenth century, these words in
retrospect seem quite prophetic as they call us to change our
relationship with animals. According to Dostoevsky, if we do
not, we go against God's purpose. And nowhere is this issue
more urgent than in our recognition of humanity's role in the
mass species extinction taking place today.

We humans have a tragic and violent history of obliter-
ating other animal species. It is a history that includes both
direct encounters of slaughter and indirect obliteration, primarily in the form of habitat destruction and the introduction
of chemicals to ecosystems. We find ourselves at the beginning
of the twenty-first century on the precipice of a worldwide
catastrophe for many other animals as their numbers dwindle
and their habitat is destroyed. How might Christians respond
to this overwhelming situation, and what is at stake?

In her powerful book *Silent Spring*, Rachel Carson, a
respected marine biologist and author, provided an early
wake-up call to the problem of species extinction resulting

from human activity.[35] Published in 1962, Carson's book responded to the impact of synthetic pesticides, most specifically DDT, on both other species and humans. In the post-World War II world, chemicals developed for wartime use were applied in increasing quantities on cropland and in heavily populated areas for insect eradication. As a small boy growing up in the late 1950s in Northern California, my husband recalls sneaking out his bedroom window to chase DDT-spraying trucks down the streets on his bicycle. He and his buddies thought that catching the spray in your face was rebellious and exciting, but even their parents were not concerned about the chemicals themselves. Newsreels had already informed the public that DDT was safe for everyone and showed children being sprayed directly with the pesticide while eating or swimming.[36]

Carson, however, warned that overuse of these new, persistent chemical pesticides could threaten life. And eventually, tragically, her warnings were confirmed. Various bird species, including the U.S. national bird, the bald eagle, experienced drastic population decline. While DDT was not solely responsible for the alarming loss of bald eagles (they had already been affected by habitat destruction), DDT's impact on the birds' ability to reproduce was hugely influential and gained national attention. By 1967 bald eagles were declared endangered in most areas of the United States. But this high-profile species, while extremely significant, does not tell the entire story.[37]

Species on the earth come and go through both slow natural processes and mass extinction events. Species adapt, are displaced, fail to reproduce, relocate, change—evolve. With incredible amounts of research, scientists have determined the background or average rates of species extinction. After establishing this average, scientists can identify the occurrence of "mass extinctions" or out-of-the-ordinary cycles. In approximately six hundred million years there have been five mass extinctions, possibly caused by climate change or the impact of a meteor. As I noted in the introduction to this chapter, at the dawn of the twenty-first century many scientists now believe that we may be entering "what could be the period of the sixth great mass extinction."[38] Just who is disappearing forever, and why? Those are difficult questions to answer definitively, but some answers are obvious.

One prominent animal in biblical stories and in the lives of saints is in desperate trouble: the whale. Many whale species are on the brink of extinction. Take the blue whale, the largest animal ever known to have lived on the earth, as a prime example: there are only 2,300 blue whales left to roam the oceans. What is to blame? The aggressive hunting for whale oil in the nineteenth and twentieth centuries led to this crisis. Commercial whaling bans have had some impact, but human development and lack of ability to enforce the moratorium on whaling means that many whale species remain on the threshold of extinction.[39] Hunting and habitat destruction alone are not the only issues.

In July 2009 Charles Siebert, an author who has researched and writes extensively about the situations of animals, published "Watching Whales Watching Us" in *The New York Times Magazine*, revealing a new and disturbing phenomenon: whales are beaching themselves, running into and getting stranded on the shore, in very high numbers. When autopsies are performed on these whales, many of them show signs of brain and ear trauma. They are hemorrhaging. In addition to this, some of the whales also have lesions on other organs, including the liver and lungs. Why? As Siebert explained, these whales are getting the "bends" (a buildup of nitrogen bubbles) from surfacing too quickly. How could this happen in ocean-diving animals like these whales?[40]

Increasing evidence points to sonar, to human-generated noises filling the ocean depths. Whales communicate over vast stretches of the ocean, so they are particularly attuned to the noise that moves through the water. As more military and commercial ships use sonar technologies, bouncing sounds around in the water until they hit something else and echo back, the ocean depths are becoming noisy, possibly deafening, to whales and other ocean creatures. Siebert in particular believes it may be so. He theorizes that these whales may be beaching themselves in desperate, ultimately suicidal, mad dashes to the ocean surface "to escape the madness-inducing echo chamber that we humans have made of their sound-sensitive habitat."[41] We are making their home uninhabitable with our noise. And we are doing so in many places, including Japan, Brazil, the U.S. Virgin Islands, and the Galapagos Islands. In each of these places, beached whales with similar lesions have been found. And in the Bahamas, where a research team studied beaked whales, a fairly small whale with a dolphin-like beak, sixteen beaching were recorded in just one week. They did not have to look too far for an explanation: testing of new sonar systems had taken place nearby. Very few whales returned after these traumatized animals died.[42]

Because of their immediate appeal, bald eagles and whales are animals who many humans are eager to save. After all, how can one imagine a world without these majestic animals in our midst? But there are other, less photogenic or popular species who are also threatened with extinction. As a matter of fact, even conservative scientific estimates indicate that humans are causing the rate of extinction to accelerate. *The*

majority of scientists agree that the current rate of species
extinction is at least one hundred times, and possibly one
thousand times, greater than the natural or background rate.
These same scientists also project that we are moving toward
an even higher rate of extinction, possibly ten thousand times
greater than at prehuman levels.[43] Species who have disappeared or are on the brink of extinction include Bengal tigers
(1,400 left in the wild), Javan rhinos (fewer than 60 remain),
and giant pandas (1,600 in the wild).[44] We might not miss
some of these animals immediately, but as humans we must
realize that our own survival depends on the flourishing of
diverse life on Earth.

Think of this: over 90 percent of animal species on the
earth are invertebrates, animals with no backbone or spinal
column. They are not necessarily cute or cuddly, but that does
not make their place on the earth unimportant. One intriguing invertebrate, for example, the veined octopus, actually
changed the way humans view this large group of animals.
In December 2009 news sources worldwide reported that
researchers investigating the little veined octopuses discovered that they were manipulating objects to make houses for
themselves. These underwater-living, multilimbed creatures
dug up coconut shells and carefully transported them as far
as 65 feet, using them as shelters.[45] This observation broke
down yet another wall of distinction between humans and
other animals; it appears that invertebrates are tool users,
a classification that has falsely set humans apart from other
animals for centuries. If current projections are substantiated,
numerous species, such as the veined octopus, could disap-
pear before we ever even know that they exist.

Habitat destruction, pollution, overconsumption of animals as resources, deliberate obliteration of species (those
usually referred to as "pests"), and simple lack of knowledge

contribute to extinction. And what is extinction all about if not the cessation of birth? How should Christians respond if humans become the agent of the end of creation—the end of God's creation?

Hospitality and Animals

The island of Assateague lines the coast of the Delmarva Peninsula, the stretch of land east of the Chesapeake Bay that includes parts of Delaware, Maryland, and Virginia.[46] This thirty-seven-mile-long barrier reef island is home to bald eagles, peregrine falcons, sika deer, fox squirrels, and bottlenose dolphins, and to over three hundred amazing wild ponies. To this day nobody knows for sure how these ponies ended up inhabiting Assateague Island. Evidence indicates that they have been there since the 1600s. Some historians suggest that a Spanish ship carrying horses to the American colonies crashed off the coast; others suggest that the ponies are descendants of horses who strayed from the various Chesapeake area settlers' free-ranging herds.[47] No humans live on Assateague Island on a permanent basis, though, at least not now. Since the middle of the twentieth century it has been a national seashore, a wildlife refuge, a place the horses can call home without worrying about human encroachment. But I grew up camping with my church youth group on Assateague. For a week every summer we would revel in the beauty of the beaches, the wildness of the dunes, and these ponies wandering in our midst. For an urban girl, sleeping in a tent with horses roaming wild around us was like a fairy tale.

Places like Assateague, though there are precious few of them now, remind us all that we humans do not own the earth. Perhaps from that perspective, some may find problematic the concept of hospitality as an ideal offered by humans. According to Christian beliefs, the earth is God's.

Assateague Island ponies. Photo by W. C. Hobgood.

But in the last several centuries, humans have, by virtue of our technologies and our expanding population, come to inhabit almost every corner of it. So, justly or not, we have, for all practical purposes, claimed the entire earth as our possession. We have taken over the homes of the many other animals who have lived here for millennia. *It is in recognition of this reality that I chose the concept of hospitality as a way to consider our relationship to animals.*

Still, what do we do with the foundational idea of orthodox Christian theology: that the earth is God's, it does not belong to us, and therefore we have no right to assume that we are the ones who should extend hospitality? When the day comes that we humans live in accordance with that truth, perhaps we can then leave hospitality to God. But the fact of the matter is this: that is simply not the way humans are living in the twenty-first century. And the reality is that we are the ones taking up all the space. Most places on the earth are under human control. If other animals are going to survive our presence, we must extend radical hospitality to them. I also wonder if we might not invert that idea as well. Might it be that for us—for humans—to survive, we must also find a way to live with other animals flourishing around us? Without this biodiversity, humans will not be here either.

It is here that the radicality of Christian hospitality enters the picture. In the contemporary world, hospitality is often narrowed to a small circle of family and friends or it is used to define an industry, and a profitable one at that. Occasionally we might include a broader group of acquaintances in the formalities of hospitality. But in the ancient and medieval worlds, hospitality was something different altogether. It was a risky business to open your space to a stranger. And it was risky to be a stranger and accept the offer. Both sides of the arrangement had something at stake. And it was the early Christians who expanded this even further.

In Christian models of hospitality, it was not only the stranger who had the ability to be in a reciprocal relationship, but also the stranger who had absolutely nothing to give in return who was welcomed. Jesus instructs his disciples, all seventy of them, to go out in pairs and be strangers who do not even carry a beggar's purse (Luke 10). As early as this, during the Jesus movement period before the formal religion of Christianity even exists, the traditional concepts of hospitality were challenged. By the time Christianity gained a foothold, stories abound providing models for the ideal of hospitality, as addressed at the beginning of this chapter. Quickly, it became a central tenet of the religion. Truly, as

Christine Pohl claims, hospitality "is a way of life fundamental to Christian identity."[48] And it is hospitality that particularly includes the neediest, the least of all.

Paul Ricoeur, one of the most distinguished philosophers of the twentieth century, interprets the "love your enemies" commandment in the gospel accounts to be "supra-ethical," as it significantly changes the prevailing golden rule (do unto others as you would have them do unto you) by not assuming reciprocity.[49] Love and hospitality are paramount regardless of the possibility of equivalent treatment. In his analysis of this idea, Alan Kirk, a scholar of the New Testament period, claims that the commandment "expresses the religious principle of the superabundance of the gift, urging emulation of God's love and mercy unilaterally bestowed on every creature without qualification."[50] In other words, one gives the gift of love and welcome knowing full well that the recipient—whether human or animal—will not be able to offer an equivalent gift in return. The extension of this gift beyond the human realm is a far-reaching ethic.

Christian hospitality extends in the same radical way as does its rethinking of the golden rule. Letty Russell, a groundbreaking theologian who was on the faculty of Yale Divinity School for years, took on hospitality for what became her final theological study. In Russell's book *Just Hospitality: God's Welcome in a World of Difference* (published posthumously), she emphasizes that concepts of hospitality must be changed to meet a changing world:

> [T]he gospel is situation variable. Knowing this is an important clue to our understanding of H. Richard Niebuhr's phrase "transforming culture." We draw our theologies out of biblical and church tradition, and we develop careful arguments for what we believe, but ultimately they have

to be seriously imaginable to people in a particular time and culture.[51]

Just as early Christians broke traditional concepts of hospitality by eating with those who were considered unclean, and just as some Christians before the Civil War broke the law by opening their homes to the Underground Railroad to help escaping slaves, so does our time call for a reexamination of the boundaries of hospitality. Other animals—those faced with the threat of extinction at our hands—must now be invited into the circle.

How will we enact this hospitality? Sometimes it will mean simply leaving spaces alone, not encroaching on the homes of other animals: leaving forests standing, wetlands intact. Other times it will involve creating spaces for animals who have already been displaced, providing sanctuaries or wilderness preserves. Regardless, the call to Christians for radical hospitality in the twenty-first century is a call that encompasses many species, not just humans.

One hopeful example can be found in the efforts of many volunteers across the world who are caring for feral cats. Cats are in a kind of threshold or liminal space in relationship to humans. Certainly the domesticated cats mentioned earlier in the book have developed in concert with human culture. But, unlike dogs, they fare well when they live on their own, at the fringes of human habitations, at the edge of human culture. All over the world cats thrive in feral colonies that are sometimes contentious for the people living around them. There are millions of these feral cats in the U.S. alone. Trap, Neuter, Release (TNR) programs are growing throughout the U.S. and the world to address the issue. Armies of volunteers help to trap these felines, take them to veterinarians, and have them vaccinated and tested for diseases and then neutered to

Author with cats at Torre Argentina Roman Cat Sanctuary in Rome. Photo by C. L. Hobgood.

prevent overpopulation, all to release them again, usually in the same place or with the same colony of cats, so they can live peacefully. The same volunteers often manage the colonies, taking turns feeding and watering the cats as well.

One magical place to see a feral colony in action is in the heart of Rome, Italy. There cats gather amid the ancient ruins of Torre Argentina. This site, excavated in the late 1920s, sits below street level, providing some safety and shelter for cats, and is close to the ancient center of the city. Almost immediately after it was excavated, cats began to gather there. For over sixty years various women given the derogatory title of *gattare* (cat ladies) fed the stray cats. During the 1990s the process was organized, funds were contributed, and the "Cats of Rome" even became something of a tourist attraction. Still, countless volunteers spend hours providing hospitality by creating a space of safety, feeding them and providing health care for them. The *gattare* understand the radicality of hospitality. They are but one superb example of compassionate hospitality for animals at work.

Other people within Christianity also understand this idea and enact it in amazing ways. Dr. Jean LeFevre, who runs a sanctuary for nonreleasable rescued wolves and wolf hybrids in east Texas, is a powerful example. In many religious traditions, Christianity included, wolves have gotten a bad rap. They represent evil in medieval Christian bestiaries and remain the "big, bad" in all too many children's tales. Yet wolves rarely pose a threat to humans and tend to stay away from us as much as possible. Nevertheless, humans have eradicated them in place after place, leaving very few safe habitats for them. That is, all but a few. LeFevre's Saint Francis Wolf Sanctuary provides a safe place for these much-maligned animals to live peacefully.

The story of Mystery, one of the sanctuary's rescued wolves, is tragic but all too typical. Mystery was born free and lived in the open spaces of Texas until, one day, she was caught in a steel leg trap—an incredibly painful way to snare an animal. While stuck in the trap, she was shot with a rifle, lost consciousness, and was probably left for dead. Yet somehow after she awoke Mystery was able to pull herself toward the sound of wolves calling, and luckily for her, these wolves were in a sanctuary. The people there found her trying to dig underneath the fence to get into the pens and rushed her to a veterinarian. After surgeries to repair her leg (she almost lost her foot), Mystery started down the road to recovery. And

Dr. Jean A. LeFevre and Mystery at the Saint Francis Wolf
Sanctuary. Photo by author.

Jean LeFavre was called to help. Because Mystery's injuries prohibited her from being safely released into the wild, LeFavre took Mystery to Saint Francis Wolf Sanctuary to live in peace and security.

While their life in the sanctuary is not as ideal as being able to run freely in the wild, Mystery and the rest of the wolves still sing, play, and bask in the sun. There are many mouths to feed, runs to clean, and veterinary bills to pay. While it is a thankless endeavor by most contemporary societal measures, LeFevre extends to these wolves the hand of radical hospitality. As she articulates so clearly, "It was never my intention to have a sanctuary for wolves and wolf-dogs. However, my experience is that there are no accidents, and even coincidences may be best described as situations in which God chooses to remain anonymous."[52]

It is this willingness to open one's heart, home, and pocketbook to the "other" that marks radical Christian hospitality, as it has for centuries. As the world changes, so do those who are the most marginalized and in need of hospitality. Most of those who extend this hand of fellowship receive more than they ever give. At least I can assure you that has been the case for me. As you know, the hands-on way that I try to embody this hospitality is through rescuing and fostering dogs in need. Dogs like Jazz (mentioned in chapter 1) and Sheba (in chapter 2) have enriched my life beyond measure. So much so that I have to wonder: might those of us who do this be entertaining angels, just as the biblical characters did so long ago? I think it just might be so.

Chapter 5

Where Have All the Animals Gone?

[W]e are united in our belief that animals have intrinsic value as part of God's creation and are entitled to live lives free of cruelty and exploitation . . . In a world of increasing violence towards others, ourselves, and our environment, we believe it is essential to reclaim and recover a commitment of compassion for all life. We believe that a commitment to compassion begins with the most vulnerable among us, which includes animals.

—*Best Friends Network*[1]

Another day when I should have been working on writing this chapter turned into a series of veterinary runs, a Petfinder photo shoot, and dog adoption coordination. I loaded Tiny, the blonde pit bull mix, and Honey, an older six-pound Chihuahua, into crates in my car; then I headed over to pick up the two mixed-breed puppies. All of these dogs were in foster homes and needed to go to the veterinarian for vaccinations and checkups. Nobody else could do it this morning, so the writing would have to wait. Tiny,

Leopold, Honey, and Riley are precious living beings, their lives mean something, they have their own intrinsic worth; I believe that with all of my heart. Along with so many other dogs and cats and orangutans and chickens, they have been disregarded by humans for too many years. I often ask myself: Why do we humans so easily close our sympathies to other animals? And it saddens me to say it, but all too often going down that road leads to religion. Time and time again

Trip, a dog who never made it out of the Georgetown Animal Shelter. Photo by J. Smith.

I see how faith traditions, Christianity included, have been a major source of this attitude of disregard and dismissal. Some of the most prevalent interpretations of beliefs in Christianity elevate the humans so far above the rest of creation that there is little if any room left for animals.

How does this happen when, as we have seen throughout the pages of this book, animals have been so prominent in the history of Christianity? Compassion-filled saints fed animals and offered them shelter; animals, in turn, fed saints out of a sense of solidarity and love. Christians and lions were taunted side by side in the Roman arenas, bearing their fate at the hands of oppression with dignity and shared conviction. Birds sang praises with Saint Francis, and fish listened to the preaching of Saint Anthony of Padua, one of Francis' first followers, who emulated his teacher's love for all creatures. The ox and the ass bowed before the manger in reverence. What has changed? And how?

It seems to me that the answer comes down to how we respond to one very basic, though undoubtedly complicated, question: *at its core, is Christianity only about human beings?* In other words, is this religious tradition almost completely human centered, as Lynn White Jr. suggested in his often-quoted and now-famous essay "The Historical Roots of our Ecological Crisis"?

> Especially in its Western form, Christianity is the most anthropocentric religion the world has seen. As early as the 2nd century both Tertullian and Saint Irenaeus of Lyons were insisting that when God shaped Adam he was foreshadowing the image of the incarnate Christ, the Second Adam. Man shares, in great measure, God's transcendence of nature.[2]

Or does Christianity have the resources to encourage the celebration and sustenance of abundant life in all of its forms, not just human?

There is certainly some ambiguity in the history of the tradition on this point, as is already apparent from discussions in earlier chapters. Over the last several hundred years, since the Enlightenment, theological ideas that place humans at the center of everything have been emphasized in a way that is out of proportion with the history of the Christian tradition. Coupled with changes in technology, science, and societal systems as a whole, this shift in the dominant Christian worldview has been, at the very least, a contributing factor to the troubled state of other animals and, at the most, a major driving force that has and continues to feed this deadly imbalance.[3]

In light of the various topics already discussed, from food to sport to endangered species to pets, let us look at three concepts that are all integral to an understanding of Christianity: the Word, sacrificial atonement, and speciesism. The Word might seem central and obvious to many Christians, but it has morphed significantly in the last five hundred years. As worship began to focus almost exclusively on preaching and less on the visual arts, popular festivals, and sacraments, animals quickly lost their place in the sanctuary. "Sacrificial atonement" is a theological concept that should be familiar to most Christians, since it relates directly to Jesus' life, death, and resurrection; it is the core of fundamental Christian beliefs about salvation. However, in my experience, while Christians too often assume it is understood, sacrificial atonement is too rarely considered thoughtfully and critically. Finally, a relatively recent articulated concept, speciesism, is simply this: the belief that one species is superior to and more valuable than all others. As I will explain below, these three ideas have combined, unintentionally perhaps, in ways that create what I call a "culture of sacrifice"—which does not bode well for animals.

The Word

My conscience is captive in the Word of God.

—Martin Luther

Animals . . . also speak in their own tongues—purring, barking, or squealing in contentment.

—Marc Bekoff[4]

The sixteenth century in Europe was a time of incredible transformation. The printing press was up and running, books and pamphlets were distributed, more and more people were learning to read. And the Protestant Reformation, in its various incarnations, was in full swing. It was a complex and intertwined series of changes that eventually led to modern Europe with its nation-states and new religious realities. And there is one aspect of this monumental shift in human culture that is particularly relevant as we ponder animals and Christianity: the increasing significance of the Word to theology, liturgy, and education.

Just what is the Word anyway, you might ask? This theological concept relates to God incarnate, or God made flesh, which connects the historical figure of Jesus of Nazareth with the cosmic concept of Christ in traditional Christian theology. According to the Gospel of John, this Word was in the beginning with God, at the creation itself. In other words, the Word, by some measure, is the form that Christ takes before Jesus is born. Some images portray a Jesus-like figure at the creation as the generative force of God. The first chapter of Genesis describes God "speaking" creation—God says,

"Let there be . . ."—and a certain strand of belief in Christianity connects this part of God to Christ.

But this concept becomes much more concrete in the theology and practice during and after the Reformation. Martin Luther (1483–1546) articulated this most clearly in his commitment to *sola scriptura* (or Scripture only). As one study of Luther explains, "The 'Word of God' was the speech of God, thus the 'God who speaks' would be an appropriate way to summarize Luther's picture of God."[5] What is the meaning of this? In short, with this new focus, if a theological belief or practice is not in Scripture, then it is not central to Christianity. So, for example, while the Roman Catholic Church for hundreds of years accepted at least seven sacraments, Protestant Reformers in the sixteenth century, under the initial leadership of Luther, claimed to only find two in Scripture. Thus only these two (communion and baptism) were deemed valid, and most Protestants still adhere to this idea. This focus on the sole authority of Scripture grew in popularity and impact as more and more copies of the Bible became available by virtue of Gutenberg's printing press. Martin Luther himself translated much of the Bible into German in order to increase its availability to the masses.

In addition, during this time worship changed dramatically. Many of the liturgical bells and whistles disappeared from Protestant sanctuaries. Both the Word as an explanation of one function of Christ and the study of scriptural texts assumed central positions in worship services throughout the Protestant world. The sacred space itself changed. Pulpits were moved to the central location in the sanctuaries, and, so as not to distract parishioners from hearing the Word as it was preached, images of the stories of saints disappeared from the walls. With other liturgical accoutrements removed, sanctuaries became spaces almost exclusively for listening to the Word. And when that happened, the animals disappeared.

Furthermore, this shift had an unexpected lasting and deep impact on Christianity's relationship to animals for another reason. While numerous scientific studies point to the existence of advanced communication systems for many other animals, most people widely believe that only humans are truly able to speak or communicate in complex ways. For example, in his incredibly influential *Discourse on Method*, René Descartes (1596–1650), one of the most important philosophers of the Enlightenment and the Scientific Revolution in Europe, argued that the "inability to use language in a fully meaningful way" is "a sign that animals 'have no reason at all.'"[6] Born at the end of the sixteenth century, Descartes inherited with its full force the Enlightenment's focus on language, and its resulting assumptions that human beings are far superior to all other forms of animal life. This connection between intelligence, human exceptionality, and language (the Word), was reinforced in new forms of Christian worship that focused almost exclusively on reading the Bible and listening to the Word as told in the form of sermons. Some great benefits of this are clear and well-known: vast increases in literacy, the development of increasingly accurate biblical translations, the availability of texts to people on a scale never before imagined, and the growth of educational systems (many of which were established in order to enable people to read the Bible), to name just a few. However, might there not also be, as with most dramatic changes, some highly significant negative consequences as well? Truly, what is the impact of considering human language as the primary, or even the exclusive, means to encounter the divine? If God is only available through the Word, not only are other animals no longer a part of the sacred system, but we cannot commune with

God in silence, in wordless action, or in nature. Imagine the
full implications of this. Many of us have experienced God
in the crashing of waves at the ocean, or in the laughter of a
toddler, or in the touch of a friend's hand, or in the smell of
a rose. All of these are devalued in relationship to the primacy
of the Word. It is, in many ways, an impoverished and narrowed sense of the divine.

Sacrificial Atonement: A Very Brief Overview

*What took place is that the Son of God fulfilled the righ-
teous judgement on us human beings by himself taking
our place as a human being, and in our place undergoing
the judgement under which we had passed . . . Why did
God become a human being? So that God as a human
being might do and accomplish and achieve and complete
all this for us wrongdoers, in order that in this way there
might be brought about by him our reconciliation with
him, and our conversion to him.*

—*Karl Barth*[7]

Karl Barth was one of the most influential theologians of
the twentieth century, and firmly embedded in his theology
is the idea of sacrificial atonement and a focus on the death
of Jesus. As Barth emphasizes elsewhere, he believed that
humans must "look directly upon Christ's cross and grave in
order to discern the truth of God's nature and the range of
divine possibility."[8] Rather than focusing on Jesus' life and
acts, Barth argued that the greatest divine truth was to be
known in Jesus' death to save sinful humans. The world was
created just for this act: to play out the drama of human salvation. Do you see what happens with this theological turn?
The entire creation of the world becomes entirely about us.
All the animals and plants created in the garden, all the manifold glories in Genesis designed for God's pleasure, become

mere and insignificant supporting actors in the human drama of falling from grace into sin and then being saved by the death of Jesus. This is the root of the turn to the human in Christianity. With all of God's attention focused on our story, there is little or no room left for any other creatures. I wonder what Behemoth and Leviathan, those two wonderful creatures who were playing with God in the book of Job, would think of that?

And then there is the notion of sacrifice on its own, which is a central and complex aspect of Christian theology. As most Christians know from phrases like the "Lamb of God," for instance, early Christians lived in a world of animal sacrifice, from those in Judaism (particularly while the Temple in Jerusalem was still standing) to the sacrifices made as part of Roman state religion.[9]

According to orthodox Christian theology, humans carry the burden of original sin, which created a chasm so wide that humans could not possibly cross it on their own. Thus, humanity's reconciliation to God had to occur on a divine scale. It was only through God's own death as a sacrifice that the sins of humanity could be overcome. Thus, through a complicated series of historical and theological interpretations in Christianity, Jesus' death comes to be understood as the ultimate replacement for animal sacrifices—and as the only sacrifice worthy enough for the salvation of a sinful and fallen humanity. This "atonement theology," with its focus on Jesus as a sacrifice to reconcile humanity to God, again places humans at the center of the divine plan. Both sacrifice and humans are now sacred.

Sacrificial atonement theology brings to the fore several questions: Are humans worthy of the sacrifice of God? Why? Did humans in some way earn this sacrifice? Certainly orthodox Christianity, even that which focuses on atonement theology, responds with a resounding "No." It is only because of the grace of God that humans are saved, and that grace shines through in the sacrifice of Jesus. But, despite that, might not this very theology still have provided the ideological framework that allowed us, over the course of more than fifteen Christian-dominated centuries in the West and, increasingly, around the globe, to elevate ourselves to a level above every other creature? And even, at least subconsciously, beyond the divine? If God so loved "the world" (meaning humans) that God gave "his only begotten Son," then surely the rest of the world (the other-than-human world) should give itself to humans as well. It is only logical, right? If humans are worth the sacrifice of God, then shouldn't all of God's creation be sacrificed to us?

It is this human-only centered theological trajectory, one that has to be seen as a bit narcissistic, that proves potentially destructive in the history of Christianity. Again, if Jesus is God (and the Son of God, in a complicated Trinitarian construction), and if God is willing to sacrifice Jesus (God) for the salvation of individual human beings, then certainly all other animals, and even some other humans, are worth sacrificing for salvation as well. Think about how prominent this is. Hymns and sermons and artwork have reinforced this idea for centuries. "Are you washed in the blood of the Lamb? Will your soul be ready for mansions bright?"[10] "What wondrous love is this that caused the Lord of bliss to bear the dreadful curse for my soul!"[11] "Jesus loves me, he who died, heaven's door to open wide."[12] Much of the popular language of Christianity, along with some of its most formative theological ideas, holds sacrificial atonement as the pivotal theological position, fundamental to the faith. As it has largely been told in recent history, the Christian system is about humans and about God. All other animals and parts of creation are excluded. Can you see what influence this has? Especially in a time when we humans also have powerful technologies that allow us to use all other parts of creation solely for our own ends? It is not at all surprising, is it, that these lowly animals suffer immensely only to end up on our plates, being inflicted with violence in our laboratories and arenas, and destroyed and discarded in our control facilities, all at our whim?

Speciesism and Christianity

Animals are not self-conscious, and are there merely as a means to an end.
The end is man.

—*Immanuel Kant*[13]

It might be an obvious statement, but the canonical biblical texts are so central to Christianity that their contested and varied interpretations carry added weight. Take, for example, the foundational creation stories—the first two chapters of Genesis. These two chapters provide fodder for almost any interpretation of the relationship of humans with all other animals. But the dominant interpretation of these stories in the history of Christianity does not necessarily bode well for animals other than humans. Unfortunately, this historically dominant interpretation does potentially provide a strong foundation for humans to be thoroughly speciesist, and it has been applied and accepted broadly for generations.

Let us look again at the first two pivotal chapters of Genesis. In the first chapter, God creates and declares everything "good." Humans are made at the end of the process and, according to the text, crafted in the divine image. In the second chapter a different story is told. God creates Adam, literally the earth being (who does not seem to have a particular gender yet in the original Hebrew texts). Then God proceeds with creating a series of animals—all of whom God hopes might prove to be suitable companions for Adam. God lets Adam name them—thus gives the human power over them—but the other animals are pronounced by God to be "good." The other animals are still not quite enough, so finally God creates the only other human, pulled famously from Adam's side. Finally, that is the right match. With the creation of the second human, the earth being (Adam) has been divided into male and female human earth beings. They have been given dominion over the rest of the garden.

Regardless of the order or the final purpose of creation, both stories contain language that lends itself to the interpretation that humans are to be at the least stewards of the creation or possibly even dominators over the rest of creation. Even though these same passages instruct humans to eat only the green plants for food, they still place humans in a relationship of superiority to all others in the garden. While later passages in the Bible raise doubts about this blanket interpretation, the position is already firmly established. According to the most prevalent interpretations in the tradition, God has deemed humans the most valuable and dominant species on the planet.

Even after the fall, with humans in need of a whole lot of redemption, in the Genesis stories and in most of Christian history, we humans remain squarely above all other animals. We are at the top of a hierarchical ladder, with only God above us. This theme can be traced easily throughout the history of the tradition, including in the works of some of the earliest Christian theologians, such as Origen, an important third-century Christian teacher in Alexandria. Origen believed that the whole of the creation was made to teach humans about salvation: "The Creator, then, has made everything to serve the rational being and his natural intelligence."[14] Even Augustine, the brilliant fourth-century theologian who wrote *The City of God* and who had a relatively positive view of creation, claimed that other animals are, by divine ordinance, "subject to our use."[15]

The trajectory continues with Thomas Aquinas, who contends that animals are, according to Divine ordinance, "preserved not for themselves but for man." With this in mind, then, "both their life and their death are subject to our use."[16] Arguably the most influential theologian of the Middle Ages, Aquinas pulls no punches when the issue of humans and animals is raised. Aquinas was determined to make the boundaries between humans and animals hard and fast, to maintain the hierarchical status quo.[17] From Origen through Augustine and Aquinas, the argument developed that there is a firm boundary between human and animal, and they, and others, began insisting upon our irreconcilable differences. These philosophical and theological strands that created distinct dualisms would heavily affect Descartes, whom we discussed earlier, and likely influenced Immanuel Kant, the influential eighteenth-century German philosopher and theologian quoted at the beginning of this section, as well.[18]

Yet even with this theological grounding existing for centuries, the sheer level of the impact of human speciesism grew by unprecedented proportions following the Enlightenment and the Scientific Revolution. While many Christian theologians throughout history argued for an extremely elevated if not unique place for humanity, the combination of this theological premise with the ideas of the Enlightenment promoted our ideas of human superiority to new extremes. Animals who had befriended saints and provided rich symbolic beauty in earlier Christianity now became mere tools. Animals ceased to be seen as living beings and came to be viewed, literally, as mere mechanical means to our desired ends. The philosopher-scientist René Descartes led the charge with his passionate and certain statements about the nature of animals:

> But there is no prejudice to which we are all more accustomed from our earliest years than the belief that dumb animals think . . . I thenceforward regarded it as certain and established that we cannot at all prove the presence of a thinking soul in animals . . . [I]t seems reasonable, since art copies nature, and men can make various automata which move without thought, that nature should produce its own automata . . . These natural automata are the animals.[19]

Certainly Descartes was not the first one to place humans at the top of the hierarchy; he had many models in the history of Western thought with its Great Chain of Being.[20] But combined with rapidly changing technologies and scientific techniques, these Enlightenment ideas impacted the lives of animals at a scale and in a way that eventually even surpassed the violence of Rome.

In her brilliant study *The Death of Nature*, Carolyn Merchant examined the fundamental changes that occurred in European culture between the sixteenth and eighteenth centuries. The new Scientific R(evolution), philosophical (Enlightenment), and economic (market capitalism) systems that emerged combined forces in ways that are often labeled "progress"—and these systems still provide the basis for modern culture. But Merchant points out that, while there have been myriad positive outcomes in the changes, there was and is a dark side to these cultural forces that is not often discussed or widely recognized. After the Enlightenment, nature could be explained scientifically, so in many ways the mystery and power were gone. Natural resources thus became the basis for rapidly growing economies; rather than sharing them in common, humans for the first time deemed nature to be owned and mined and, in large part, controlled by the wealthiest of people. Animals, along with the rest of nature, became commodities rather than subjects with a life. In short, a price tag could be put on everything (arguably even humans as a paid labor force, and not well paid at that), and all of nature became a product for consumption or a source of revenue—with no deeper meaning or value. Animals were no longer the bearers of divine messages; Balaam's ass and his kin became fairy tales when once they had been agents of God. Nature and all of her animals became machines; gaining heaven was left for only humans, and not for all of them at that.

By the nineteenth century, as increasing numbers of people moved into urban areas and away from the rural landscape, they encountered fewer animals in their daily lives. As is the case for many people today, living animals were rarely known before being slaughtered and eaten. Only a few domesticated animals, pets, remained visible in the everyday lives of most humans. The "wild" animals were considered exotic and were eventually displayed as objects in zoos or circuses. Even animals who once worked alongside humans shifted categories; horses became hobbies for the wealthy, and the "pet" dog became a cultural fixture for the middle class.

In the cityscape and the landscape, machines literally replaced animals. The "horseless carriage" filled the streets, and the horse disappeared. Plows were no longer pulled by oxen. In many cases this was a good thing for some of the animals; the lives of beasts of burden were rarely pleasant. But it was another step in the process of removing real animals from the lives of humans. Humans became an isolated species with animals hidden in the margins. Toy animals such as hobbyhorses and teddy bears filled the niche for children, but they were a sad substitute for the real, living creature.

By the late twentieth century, animals were mostly cartoons, appearing on television as mere shadows of their real selves.

Eventually philosophers, theologians, historians, and ethicists started to ask questions about what it meant for humans to be so removed from other animals in daily life. So much of human culture had developed around animals and included reflections about them. Animals were understood to be both like us and different from us; they had held deep meaning. They served as guides to the afterlife (as dogs had so often been), as symbols for the divine (such as the dove in Christianity), as healers or saints themselves. As John Berger, an art historian who studies images of animals in human culture, states so eloquently, "Animals first entered the imagination as messengers and promises." They constituted "the first circle of what surrounded man . . . They were with man at the center of his world."[21]

Based in part on these reflections about the growing divide between humans and animals, the word "speciesism" entered the vocabulary. Speciesism was coined by Richard Ryder, a British philosopher and psychologist, in the early 1970s. Ryder used speciesism to describe the "widespread discrimination" practiced by humans against all other species.[22] It can be paralleled with sexism, racism, and other more commonly acknowledged prejudices. As speciesists, humans understand ourselves to be not only the primary but the sole ultimate concern. All other animals (and plants and indeed the whole earth) are subordinated to our needs and wants. On the surface one might think that this is the way all species function, with their own survival as the primary motivator for what they do. But from what we can tell by carefully observing numerous other animals, humans are the only speciesists around. Other animals kill for food and to defend territory, to be sure. But they do not seek out other animals simply to kill them for undetermined or less than necessary reasons. While other animals share their space, we humans seem to have difficulty doing so.

With our twenty-first-century scientific and technological prowess, humans also have the ability to impact other species to a degree previously unimagined. We thoughtlessly, or sometimes deliberately, decide that another animal or species is inconvenient and determine ways to rid ourselves of it (as we almost did with wolves). Or we discover that another animal is particularly profitable and figure out ways that we can use it, often so quickly that we decimate it (as was the case with the bison in the nineteenth century).[23] Numerous examples of both of these tragic outcomes and more were addressed in chapter 4.

Speciesism is bolstered by religious ideas that, along with economic and political systems, allow it to thrive and embed itself deeply in human culture. If a religion is focused only on the salvation of individual human beings, as many forms of Christianity are, then the lives and fates of other animals can seem inconsequential. If the world is only a stage on which humanity works out its salvation, other animals no longer matter. As we have seen throughout this chapter, Christianity can lean in this direction, sometimes unabashedly and deliberately. But, as I have hinted throughout this book and will address more fully below, Christianity can also confront speciesism directly, calling into question its very foundations.

Recently some of the same scientific techniques and ideas that helped to promote speciesism for decades are now being used to challenge its assumptions. Researchers are constantly uncovering evidence of culture and intelligence in a variety of nonhuman species. Labels used to mark human exceptionalism have fallen by the wayside. Once considered to be the only users of tools, we know now humans are just one group among many tool users. Even invertebrates use tools, as underscored by recent observations of small squids building houses from coconut shells.[24] Humans were also once considered the only species to exhibit self-awareness, but elephants, dolphins, and several other primates recognize themselves in the mirror, a primary way to test this idea of "the self." Even the belief that humans are the only bearers of culture is in question. Recent reports on dolphins, for example, suggest that they "have distinct personalities, a strong sense of self and can think about the future." In addition, they are "cultural" animals, since "new types of behavior can quickly be picked up by one dolphin from another." Dolphins can "solve difficult problems, while those living in the wild cooperate in ways that imply complex social structures and a high level of emotional sophistication."[25] And for years we have known that chimpanzees have culture; different groups use different tools or processes for the same task, then pass this knowledge along to their offspring. And, as mentioned in chapter 1, scientists now believe that other communal animals may even have a sense of justice or morality.[26]

Yes, Christianity has played a great role in strengthening the idea that humans are not only unique but superior to other animals and, most likely, the only animal that matters or has any inherent value. This human exceptionalism is so ingrained in Christianity that I suspect even using the phrase "nonhuman animal" might seem a bit awkward or unseemly for many Christians. In the same way that many feminist theologians have asked if a religion centered on the idea of God becoming a male human being could ever empower women, so many ecological theologians have asked if a religion based on God becoming a human being at all could ever empower the rest of the animals in creation.

When God is literally pictured as human and as a male human in almost two thousand years of a religious tradition, it tends to reinforce the idea that humans are also at the top of the Great Chain of Being. This critique has been fleshed out by numerous ecofeminist theologians, including Sallie McFague, Rosemary Radford Ruether, Heather Eaton, Elisabeth Schussler Fiorenza, and Lois Lorentzen (just to name a few), so I will not elaborate fully here. However, as we discuss the idea of the "culture of sacrifice" below, it will be important to keep in mind the problematic possibility that Christianity's basic story may itself reinforce speciesism.

A Culture of Sacrifice: A Look at Christianity and Animals in the Twenty-First Century

Chapter 3, "Eating Mercifully: Animals for Food," opened with a quotation from one of Martin Luther's sermons on Jesus' Sermon on the Mount. Though it comes to us from the sixteenth century, I want to begin this section with a portion of that sermon that is, I think, quite insightful and possibly even prophetic:

> All animals live in contentment and serve God, loving and praising Him. Only the evil, villainous eye of man is never satisfied . . . Nor can it ever be really satisfied because of its ingratitude and pride. It always wants the best place at the feast as the chief guest (Luke 14:8). It is not willing to honor God, but would rather be honored by God.[27]

In this sermon, preached in the early sixteenth century, Martin Luther cuts to the heart of humanity's self-centered tendencies. And even more so, Luther points to the weakness of a theological system that elevates humanity beyond the point of our own significance. Isn't this fascinating, given his emphasis on the Word and the consequences of that emphasis within Christianity as a whole? Maybe Luther was not as wedded to humans' superiority as it seems? Or perhaps, at least, not as wedded to it as are the inheritors and redactors of many of his ideas.

In the early twenty-first century, the Word (understood as human exceptionality through the symbol of rational speech), sacrifice, and speciesism take on a variety of new meanings, meanings that have been accumulating and transforming these concepts for at least the last century and, more likely, for the last millennium. Not only are animals used in scientific and medical research literally called "sacrifices" when they die as a result of the research, but the less explicitly named practices of contemporary culture rely on the sacrifice of exponentially more animals than at any time or any place in human history. Whether these are entire species driven to extinction by humanity's expansion onto more and more land or entire species produced at artificially high numbers for human meat consumption, contemporary U.S. culture engages in animal sacrifice at a staggering level. Specific numbers are cited in each of the chapters in this book, but I hope that you too now see that the combined idea and reality of these facts is alarming. We humans count ourselves worthy of the sacrifice of huge, unprecedented numbers of animals. It is horrifying to see how some of the central ideas of Christianity might be propping up this system, leading us down the road toward and justifying this culture of sacrifice. This potentially deadly trajectory of Christian theology, paired with the European American technological-scientific and economic systems of power, has the potential to lead us, in short course, to the eve of destruction.

Sacrifice at the altar of science might be the most telling example to consider. I was taken aback the first time I heard a scientist call the rats she used for research "sacrifices." When

I asked why that particular term was used and if she had ever considered it a religious designation, she was struck by the question with the same kind of force that had hit me. It had not crossed her mind that the language is religious. Science and its methods are usually considered to be totally secular pursuits. But there is a belief system based on an understanding of humans as superior that allows for our use of millions of animals as "sacrifices" in scientific laboratories.

Animals are used for a variety of kinds of scientific experimentation—education, biomedical research, and product testing (from cosmetics to household cleaners). Some of these forms of experimentation are more controversial and difficult to address than others. And while it is difficult to know exactly how many animals are used in the United States each year for experimental purposes, knowing at least a few of the basic statistics is helpful in order to understand the scope of this issue.

According to the Animal Care Annual Report of Activities provided by the USDA, 1,027,450 animals were used in research in the United States in the year 2007.[28] This figure includes dogs, cats, guinea pigs, rabbits, primates, farm animals, hamsters, and the ambiguous "all other covered species" category. The uncovered species, mice and rats, are not included in this report; it is difficult to know exactly how many of these small mammals are used in research facilities, but estimates range from twenty to twenty-five million per year.

At Southwestern University, the institution where I teach, rats are one of the main animals used for research. For one academic year I served on the university's Institutional Animal Care and Use Committee. Required by federal regulations, this committee oversees the use of animals in research. These committees at research institutions nationwide ask some very basic questions: Are the animals kept in safe and

sanitary conditions? Is the research necessary in order to gen-
erate new knowledge (not just for practice, for example)?
Is there an alternative to using animals? It was one of the
most emotional and difficult committee assignments I ever
had, but I knew that it was necessary for me to walk into the
world of biomedical research before I could write about it.
One of my former students, an animal behavior major who
struggled with the work she had to do in the laboratories,
work that included sacrificing rats, wrote a powerful piece
of poetry reflecting on her experiences. It was dark, haunt-
ing, and disturbing; in the end, there was little I could say
in response to the profound words of a twenty-one-year-old
science student struggling with a belief system based around
a culture of sacrifice.

I do not deny that the issues surrounding animal sacrifice
in experimentation are complicated. Biomedical experiments
on animals might save human lives; some scientists claim that
they have. However, other scientists claim that such experiments might actually impede discovery. But, from what I can
glean after walking into laboratories and reading about these
experiments, biomedical research is still conducted at a rate
that is beyond what is necessary and for purposes that are
controversial to say the least.[29]

Some humans have started to ask where the lines should
be drawn, at least when we consider other primates. I took
this into account when visiting a facility that houses primates
used in biomedical and veterinary research and recorded my
impressions:

> A group of chimpanzees stare at my colleague as he skill-
> fully tosses graham crackers to them for a midday snack.
> Over 150 chimpanzees, and countless other smaller

primates, live at this research facility not far from Austin, Texas.[30] It is affiliated with the University of Texas' cancer research and veterinary programs and is one of only nine biomedical and research laboratories in the United States that still use chimpanzees in research. These nine centers house approximately 1000 chimpanzees, some of whom were caught in the wild and have been in these facilities for over forty years. Several of the chimpanzees knew exactly what to do to get their graham cracker. One female folded her lower lip down making a pitiful face. Another one climbed high on the apparatus in the middle of the yard and clapped her hands. They all knew exactly what was happening as this person who has been interacting closely with them for years came with a treat that day. It is difficult to look at these, the closest genetic relatives to humans, without seeing them as so like us. Their faces, their hands, their gestures, their gazes are so very "human," for what that is worth.[31]

Because of this similarity, chimpanzees do have numerous human advocates trying to make sure that they are treated well, and in comparison to many other animals, there are relatively few of them in research captivity. We might be approaching the end of the research process involving chimpanzees in the United States. Though for the squirrel monkeys and rhesus macaques whom I met in central Texas, life will likely still end in sacrifice.

Indeed, for Kant the end is man, while Luther questions this end and wonders whether or not we humans merely honor ourselves. Yet other theologians, myself included, think there is a more compassionate foundation to Christianity. At its core, is this not a religion of compassion and of justice for all of God's creatures?

At Last, the Answer to the Question

If there is no God for thee,
Then there is no God for me.

—*Anna Hempstead Branch*[32]

After now reading nearly this entire book, and after hearing what is hopefully relevant information from the history
of Christianity, how do you think this central, most imperative question should be answered: *at its core, is Christianity
only about human beings?* Despite all that you have read,
and all the creeds, texts, theologies, and stories in the long
tradition of Christianity, I suspect to some extent, as with
all matters of faith, the answer for each of us ultimately may
come down to what we each know to be true from our own
experience. When my wonderful border collie mix Beaugart,
whom I spoke of in the first chapter, died, I was unable to
function for several days. Finally I did something that I had
never done before and have not done since: I kept a journal. And Anna Hempstead Branch's short poem "To a Dog"
graced the opening page. The question she raises is central to
my understanding of Christianity.

After grappling with it for years, first as a child raised in
the church and now as an adult who thinks and teaches about
the Christian tradition, the answer seems amazingly straightforward to me. Careful study of the history of the Christian
tradition leads me to so many resources for a theology of
compassion for and connection to animals. Throughout the
history, these sources, many of which have been scattered
through the pages of this book, affirm the God this poem
suggests: a God who cares about all life on this planet—
human, canine, feline, ape, fish, insect. At its core, Christianity is a religion of compassion, of solidarity, of hospitality, of
communion, and of justice. All of these foundational ideas,

expressed earliest in the stories of Jesus and repeated throughout history in the lives of myriad saints and common people,
extend beyond one's immediate family, community, and, yes,
I firmly believe, beyond one's own species.

Albert Schweitzer (1875–1965), a Christian theologian
who received the Nobel Peace Prize for his ideas regarding a
"reverence for life," argued that one is holy if one

> . . . does not ask in what way this or that form of life mer-
> its or does not merit sympathy as something valuable . . .
> Life as such is holy . . . When working by candlelight on
> a summer night, he would rather keep the windows closed
> and breathe stuffy air than see insect after insect fall on
> the table with wings that are singed. If he walks along the
> street after rain and notices an earthworm which has lost
> its way he reflects that it must shrivel up in the sun if it does
> not wriggle in time into the earth, and so he carries it from
> the death-dealing stones to the grass. If he comes upon an
> insect that has fallen into a puddle, he takes time to extend
> a leaf or a reed to save it. He is not afraid of being smiled
> at as a sentimentalist.[33]

The core of Christianity, as Schweitzer understands it, is
compassion and the understanding that all life is sacred. A
religion of compassion is one based on an ethic of care, sympathy, and empathy, maybe even sentimentality in its best
expressions.

Every animal, including humans, whom God created and
continues to create is sacred to God. This seems to be clearly
articulated throughout the biblical texts and in the lives of so
many saints told throughout the pages of this book. Actually,
this is also traditional Christian incarnational theology at its
most radical and inclusive.[34] If God is incarnated in Jesus,
does that event point to God's incarnation in all bodies and
all creatures? With this deep concept of divine incarnation

undergirding the tradition, Christianity is necessarily a religion of compassion; because we are all, humans and others, connected to and in relationship with each other, the God exemplified by this incarnation embodies an ethic of care.

One of the main challenges to Christians, then, in the twenty-first century is this: how do we extend this theology of care and compassion to animals? There have been several concrete examples provided in the preceding pages, and there are more specific ones offered in the Additional Resources. It is important to keep in mind that these are embodied examples of a complex theological underpinning, but that is what a Christian ethic of care requires. While Christianity has historically been a religion of orthodoxy (of right beliefs), when issues of compassion are paramount, it must function as a religion of orthopraxy (of right practice). Right Christian practice in the contemporary world, with the many suffering animals in our midst, calls us to alleviate that suffering and to extend compassion, hospitality, and mutual relationship to all of God's creatures.

Closing Vision for Animals and Humans

Crowds gather hours in advance for the annual blessing of animals at the Cathedral Church of Saint John the Divine in New York City. People with their cats, parrots, turtles, snakes, dogs, and hamsters in tow congregate for the celebration of the Feast of Saint Francis, with its accompanying blessing. Many of the animals are happy to be there. The white mixed-breed senior dog appears perfectly content in the baby stroller as the elderly woman strokes her little canine companion's head. She tells me that they had attended this service together for sixteen straight years and attributes her dog's longevity to the blessing. A fabulous Weimaraner grins and wags as his people show him off to the crowd. Even the amazingly calm pair of ferrets perched on human shoulders seem at ease with the gathering. Of course a couple of relatively annoyed cats might have been happier staying at home. But overall the creatures, both human and other, are beaming, happily anticipating the one day each year when the sanctuary of this massive gothic church opens up to all of them.[35] The whole scene is reminiscent of a twenty-first century urban Noah's ark.

Group Discussion Guide

1. What was most surprising to you in this book: the stories of the saints and other places that nonhuman animals appeared in the Christian tradition, or the contemporary plight of animals in our culture?

2. Before reading this book, how aware were you of the realities today of companion animals? What about animals used for sports? Animals bred for food? Animals used for experiments? If you knew about their plight, how did you come to learn of it?

3. Do you think it is possible for humans to encounter God through their interaction with animals? Why or why not? Have you had a relevant personal experience?

4. What do you think about the possibility that other-than-human animals have emotional lives and self-awareness? How much in common do you think we humans have with the rest of the animal kingdom? Does this affect how you conceive God?

5. Do you know of a congregation that has included animals in any type of worship service? If so, what did you

hear about it? Was it well received? Can you imagine attending such a service yourself? If so, what would you think of it?

6. Is it important for contemporary Christians to know the stories of early martyrs, such as Thecla, and of the saints, such as Roch? Why or why not? Which, if any, would you like to know more about?

7. Have you ever before considered the connections between eating and religion? Do you agree that everything you choose to eat could be a religious decision? If so, what would that mean?

8. How did you react to the book's discussion of hunting? What do you think about the Safari Club and other sport hunting groups that brand their programs as Christian endeavors?

9. Thinking of science and laboratory experiments in particular, what do you think Christianity has to say about animal sacrifice? Who can or should be sacrificed? Who should decide? And where would you draw the line?

10. As you saw in this book, Christianity has changed and evolved over time. How much do you think it can change and still be Christianity? What is unchangeable?

11. Do you think Christians and the church are ready to step forward to help the rest of animals in creation? If so, in what ways? If not, what do you think it will take to engage Christians in this issue? Or, do you think it is an inappropriate issue for Christians to engage?

12. Having read this book, will you now change anything in your daily life? If so, what?

How to Help
Ideas for Individuals and Households

I am often struck by the sense of helplessness that people can feel after opening their hearts and minds to animals and all of the issues related to them. Extinction is so permanent, and habitat loss seems out of our control. There are so many dogs and cats at the shelter; it is so hard to look at their faces and leave without taking every single one of them home with us. The factory farming system is so massive, where do we even begin?

But when it comes to our relationships with animals, a plethora of ways are available for individuals and small groups of people to make a huge difference. And, as we say in the dog rescue world, we might not be able to help them all, but we can save "one dog at a time." Here are a few suggestions of some things you can do, maybe just one day, and just one animal, at a time.

Companion Animals

For many of you, working with companion animals might be the single most immediate and rewarding possibility. There are municipal and private shelters in every community nationwide, literally thousands of them. Simply do a Google search for your city or county, and you will find the local animal control facility. Some of these are able to provide more humane and stable conditions than others; the difference is primarily based on funding provided by the municipality and education of the community at large. However, I have rarely heard of an animal shelter that did not welcome volunteers. The tasks are endless: walking dogs, cleaning cat cages, organizing fund-raisers, providing adoption counseling, fostering sick animals, spreading the word about homeless pets, working with local schools to educate children, taking animals to nursing homes for visits, and advocating for pets to be spayed or neutered. If you wonder what your local shelter needs, just ask. Sometimes if you present a good idea, and are willing to follow through with it, you can begin a whole new program and benefit countless pets.

Another way that you can help is to inform friends and family about the horrors of puppy mills. Large pet stores with multiple breeds of puppies have usually purchased those puppies from "puppy brokers." These puppy brokers buy the puppies from large-scale puppy production facilities commonly referred to as puppy mills. The puppies that are born there are often not healthy, and these operations contribute to a huge overpopulation problem. However, the breeding mother dogs have it worst of all. They are bred over and over again, and many never even touch the ground. Most are kept their entire lives in small wire "rabbit cages" suspended above the ground.

As often-repeated pet advocates' mottos say, "Don't buy while shelter animals die," and "Save a life, spay and neuter your pet." Encourage family and friends to adopt homeless pets instead of purchasing them. One of the best resources for finding homeless pets is one that I've mentioned already, Petfinder (http://www.petfinder.com/). It provides an easy-to-navigate search function with location, age, type of pet, and more listed.

Another way you can help is to give some homeless pets a lift one weekend. Countless dogs and cats often need to be transported from one location to another in order to get to a rescue group or to a new permanent home. These "rescue runs" happen day in and day out all over the country, especially from the south (where spay and neuter policies are not strong) to the north (where laws are enforced and pet population is better under control). Without these transports, countless animals with a newfound hope would never get their new beginnings. To find out more about this, watch the wonderful documentary *Fifteen Legs* (http://www.fifteenlegs.com/documentary.html).

And finally, you can contribute to pet food banks and assist with temporarily homeless pets, especially during economic hard times. When people lose their jobs, become homeless, or experience domestic violence, they often face very difficult decisions about what to do with their beloved pets. Studies indicate, for example, that people who are victims of domestic violence sometimes delay leaving a dangerous situation because they are unable to take a pet with them to safety. So start to think of ways you can help to alleviate these tragic situations that link human and animal suffering, and be prepared to jump in to help when crisis strikes.

Animals as Food

The single greatest impact we each have on the largest number of animals is our consumption of meat. Personally, because of these realities, I am a vegan; however, one does not need to become a complete vegetarian or vegan to make a huge difference. A diet that consists primarily of fruits, grains, and vegetables is a much healthier one. So perhaps begin by focusing on one meat-free day each week, and remember that this was a standard practice throughout Christian history (meatless Fridays, those days that have shifted to fish fries during Lent, a much modified version). Eventually this might increase to two or three days a week.

If there are reasons that make it difficult or problematic to decrease your meat consumption, locate a local, humane rancher and purchase meat as a "locavore." The local food movement is growing rapidly and has started to replace the organic movement as a sustainable choice. One place where you can find information about more humane meat options is Humane Farm Animal Care (http://www.certifiedhumane .org/).

Animals in Sport

Unless you actively participate in betting on thoroughbred horse racing or dogfighting (a relatively small group of people), how can you impact the lives of animals who are used for "sport"? As mentioned for each issue, one of the most effective avenues is being an advocate and educator. And one issue that requires a whole lot of education is the use of pit bulls for dogfighting. Through no fault of their own, these dogs are exposed to incredible violence today in the United States. Different "bully breeds" come and go in terms of popularity (Rottweilers, boxers, bulldogs, Staffordshire terriers, Dobermans, and more), but many of these dogs end up in shelters because people do not understand their personalities. They also are disproportionately represented in shelters because they are overbred. And once there, they rarely make it out. And when they do, one has to worry if they are going to a good home or to an amateur fighting rink. Educate yourself on this type of dog and help create networks for them in your area. One of the best sites to find accurate information is BAD RAP (http://www.badrap.org/).

Species Extinction

With pets and with food choices, there are ideas listed above that provide an immediate way to engage with and impact an issue. Helping to prevent species extinction is, obviously, much more complicated. But there are some small-scale ways that individuals can affect this extinction crisis. First, if you have a yard, investigate ways to make that space more accommodating to native plant and animal species. Pollinator gardens are an easy way to start. The U.S. Fish and Wildlife Service has a simple guide online that walks you through the steps for attracting these important species (http://www.fws.gov/Pollinators/PollinatorPages/YourHelp.html). As a consumer, the choices you make can also make a great difference. For example, purchasing products crafted from sustainably harvested wood helps to preserve rain forest habitat. Millions of acres of rain forest are leveled each year both for wood use and to create grazing land for cattle.

If you eat fish, check to make sure it is sustainably caught. Years ago the idea of "dolphin-safe tuna" became very popular, and cans of tuna are still labeled with a dolphin-safe symbol. In a world where the fish population is rapidly depleting (thus the fisheries and the many people whose livelihoods depend on them are being depleted as well), selecting which fish you will eat can have a major impact. As of early 2010, these are some popular fish species still fairly abundant and being caught or farmed sustainably: European anchovies, U.S. catfish, Pacific halibut, mullet, farmed oysters, wild Alaskan salmon, farmed striped bass, and farmed rainbow trout. At the same time, the list of fish to avoid in order to help the species recover includes Chilean sea bass, king crab, Atlantic flounder/sole, grouper, orange roughy, farmed or Atlantic salmon, shark, red snapper, and more. For a complete list, go to the Environmental Defense Fund's Seafood Selector (http://www.edf.org/page.cfm?tagID=1521); this site also includes alternative fish selections and good recipe suggestions.

How to Help
Ideas for Communities and Congregations

Any community or congregation has so much that it can offer simply because of the number of ears that are available to hear and the number of hands that can be drawn upon to help. Below I offer some suggestions for activism for groups and then examples of liturgies and blessings that can be incorporated into the community's religious services.

Ideas for Activism

1. Contact your local animal shelter and have a small group (perhaps a Sunday school class) volunteer to help with any events they need. Or your group could visit the animals at the shelter and take a blessing to them.

2. Contact your local domestic violence shelter to see if they have a program in place to house the pets of people who are at the shelter. If not, try to coordinate short-term housing for these pets.

3. Feature one pet at the local shelter every month in the community's newsletter. Sponsor the animal until it finds a permanent home.

4. Create a pet food bank for families in need.

5. Write letters as a congregation to your senators and con-gresspeople and ask them to sponsor and support laws against animal cruelty and that require pets to be spayed and neutered.

6. Organize a once-a-month compassionate meal. Publish the recipes on your personal or organizational website, or post them on your facebook page. (And eventually you could gather up enough recipes to publish a com-passionate cookbook to fund your pet food bank and other efforts!)

7. Coordinate a farmers' market at your church for those who farm humanely and sustainably. Or search out where you can find those products, and inform others in the community.

8. Divide up and investigate which cosmetics, hair prod-ucts, lotions, toiletries, and cleaners are manufactured by companies that perform experiments on animals and which do not. Compile a list and publish it on the church's website, and share with the wider community.

9. Schedule showings and discussions of the documentaries *Food, Inc.*; *Fifteen Legs*; and the HSUS's *Eating Merci-fully*. Add this book, and others on animal issues, to the congregation's reading list.

10. Commit to spreading the word about the situation of animals, first within the church (perhaps through a spe-cial class) and then to those in your community. Most people have no idea.

Liturgical Resources

One of the most public ways that a congregation can display concern for other animals is through liturgy. Blessings of ani-mals can take many forms and can focus on different issues.

Here are just a few ideas about ways you can incorporate blessings of animals into your congregation's life.

———

Annual Blessing of Pets at the Feast of Saint Francis

Celebrations of this popular festival are growing in the U.S. among Catholics and Protestants alike. The feast of Saint Francis is held on October 4 each year. Most congregations select the Saturday or Sunday closest to that date to hold the blessing. AmericanCatholic.org gathers a listing of many of the blessings held in each state on its website (http://www .americancatholic.org/features/francis/US.asp). While it is not a complete listing, it is the most comprehensive one I have yet found. Online one can find many outlines of services for pet blessings. Included below is a basic liturgy for a blessing of pets that I have used several times, and compiled from several sources or written the text myself.[1]

As with any worship event, there are a couple of logistical considerations. The first is finding the most appropriate setting. This service can be held inside the church, outside in the parking lot, on the church steps, or in a local park. I find it to be a powerful statement to bring pets into the church sanctuary itself, but if that becomes a hurdle (as it might in some congregations), then holding the blessing outside is fine and works well. The second consideration is educating the congregation about what will happen. You'll need to give specific instructions and create a flyer that can be shared with friends who might want to attend as well. These instructions should include basic safety and consideration hints, such as the following: keep all small pets in safe travel containers, keep all dogs leashed, and make sure all animals are fully vaccinated. Pets who prefer to be away from other animals should be left at home. Ask people to take their own pet into consideration—would she or he really like to come to this public event, or would it be too stressful for them? For those animals who will not attend, individual blessings can be offered in their homes.

Introduction

God created the animals—birds of the air, fish of the sea, and the many beloved creatures who walk or crawl on the earth—and God declared them all to be good. The glory of a horse running, the beauty of an eagle in flight, the majesty of a dolphin leaping: all display the wonder of sacred life. We are gathered here today to bless the animals that are in our midst, those who are our very close companions, and to ask for God's blessing on these friends and on the many animals who share this earth with us.

We are also here to repent, to recognize that, as powerful animals ourselves, we do not always live kindly with all of God's creatures. We pray that this time together, a time of recognition of the gifts and worthiness of every living being, will remind us that all life is precious to God.

Prayer for God's Creatures

Let us pray.

Life-giving Creator of all, we ask your blessing on every animal gathered here today, the ones with two legs or four, the large and the small, the furry and the fluffy, the barking and the squawking. May they live joyfully and peacefully, praising you as they live out the lives you intended for them. Bless us all to love your creation and revere its sacredness. Give the humans present the gift of compassion, with eyes to see suffering and hearts that strive to end it. We ask this blessing in the name of the one who was, is, and always will be our Creator, to whom every creature belongs.

Scripture Reading

Any number of Scriptures work here: Genesis 1:20-25; Isaiah 11:6-9; Job 12:7-10; and Proverbs 12:10.

Brief Meditation on Scripture

This could reflect on the role of animals in our lives. I have also told stories of animals and saints from the history of the tradition.

Hymn

Some appropriate hymns are "For the Beauty of the Earth," "All Creatures of Our God and King," and "All Things Bright and Beautiful."

Blessing of All the Pets

God, our Creator, we ask you to bless our pets with your light and love.

Make our animal friends safe, happy, healthy, and whole.

Help us to better understand as we learn from our animal friends' wisdom, from their innocence and their loyalty.

Help us model their ability to forgive, to not judge human beings unkindly.

As we bless these animal companions today, we thank you for the pleasures, the humor, the delight and smiles they bring to our lives.

Thank you for their companionship and friendship, especially when they stay with us during those lonely hours we may have experienced.

Thank you for our companions' natural ability to teach us to be aware of the present moment.

Thank you for the pure beauty of every animal—their forms, colors, textures, motions are all a work of art, and may we appreciate your creation of this masterpiece.

Bless all animals in harm's way, heal the sick, protect those who are lost, and guide them to safety. Thank you for the gift of love. Amen.

Individual Blessings

Now we ask that you each bring your pet forward for an individual blessing. After the blessing may you travel safely home together.

> *[Invite each individual animal forward. If there is a large gathering, separate the group into different lines for individual blessings.]*

As each pet comes forward, say the following:

Blessed are you, Lord God, maker of all living creatures. You called forth fish in the sea, birds in the air, and animals on the land. You inspired Saint Francis to call all of them his brothers and sisters. We ask you to bless this pet. By the power of your love, enable this beloved creature to live according to your plan. May we always praise you for all your beauty in creation. Blessed are you, Lord our God, in all your creatures! Amen.

> *[You can also hand out a small Saint Francis medallion, a dog treat, or other symbols at this point.]*

Blessing of Farm or Food Animals

I admit that this will be more controversial, but a blessing of the farm or food animals is an important kind of blessing to consider. Just because it makes us uncomfortable does not mean that the animals are less deserving of a blessing. Before doing so, however, I recommend that all participants be educated about the process through which meat gets to the store and to your plate in the U.S. today. Reading chapter 3 would be good preparation.

Again, consider logistics: do you know a local farmer or rancher who would let you come to her/his farm to interact with animals? In that case, you would probably be meeting animals who are living a much better life than the ones in the factory farming system (and that should be made clear to all participants), but it would get you in proximity to real animals. Alternatively, you could go to a feedlot where animals are actually prepared for the factory farming system. To locate feedlots, you can contact the U.S. Environmental Protection Agency office in your state (http://www.epa.gov/epahome/regions.htm). Nebraska, Oklahoma, Texas, Colorado, and Kansas, for example, are much more likely to have feedlots than other states.

Opening Prayer

God, we thank you for the many gifts of food that you give to us—fruits, vegetables, grains, grasses. Today we particularly want to focus on the many animals that humans eat. We know that sometimes they are not treated well when they are alive, and we are sorry for that. Please help us be more merciful, more aware, and genuinely compassionate to these animals.

Scripture Reading

Genesis 1:24-31; Isaiah 11:6-9

Reflection on Reading

In the first chapter of Genesis, God gives the green plants to humans and to all the other animals for their food. This is the idea of the peaceable kingdom, echoed again in the Isaiah passage. Later, in Genesis 9, after the flood, God gives humans the animals for food as well. But there is a price we pay. God tells Noah that the rest of the animals will fear and dread us from that point forward. We lost the peaceable kingdom, we lost the garden, the animals are afraid of us now. And rightfully so. How can we restore this peace again? At the very least, we can treat the animals that we eat with kindness and give them lives that are full and rich. Then, when it is time to kill them for our food, we can do so with compassion, in a way that will minimize their suffering.

Confession of Sin

Leader: God, we know that we can be inhumane to the rest of your animals.

People: Please forgive us, God.

Leader: To all of the animals here, we are sorry for our lack of compassion.

People: Please forgive us, God. Please forgive us, all you animals who belong to God.

Leader: God, we know that we think the animals belong to us, when they really are yours.

People: Forgive us for our lack of humility.

Leader: God, we will do our best to spread kindness and peace throughout your creation. Amen.

Blessing of the Animals

We are gathered here in the midst of these _____ (name the farm or food animals) today to remember that they are also children of God. To all of the animals in our midst and to all of the animals you represent for us, we ask God to grant you peace, to grant us a heart of compassion, and to make your lives on this earth joyful and just. Amen.

Blessing of Endangered Species

In the same manner as the blessing of food/farm animals, blessing endangered species requires both some preceding education and logistical planning. If there are endangered species habitats anywhere close to where you are located, it would be helpful to know that and to go as close to that area as possible. It is probably best not to actually enter the area with endangered species; oftentimes that is even illegal, and it is certainly not good for the endangered species in many cases. But knowing of their presence in proximity to you is a good educational practice.

Another option is to find out what species might have lived where you are located but are now extinct there. This might take some research, but it is also helpful information to know and to share with the broader community.

Opening Prayer

Creator God, you fashioned the heavens, the earth, and the waters, filling them all with creatures whom you proclaimed to be good. We confess that we have not always listened to your words of wisdom and, as a species, we have used more than our share. Today we gather to thank you again for the majestic creatures that you put on the earth. We ask you for guidance to keep us from destroying them.

Scripture Reading

Job 39

Reflection on Reading

In this passage, God is responding to Job. Many people are familiar with the story. Job is the most faithful of people. Still, God decides to test his faith. Job loses everything and, through most of the process at least, does not complain. Finally, Job yells at God because of all that he has lost. Job 39 is part of God's reply. In this passage God is reminding Job, and all humans, that we are not the center of everything that is. Rather, God has fashioned fabulous animals, and we are called upon to recognize that. God is the Creator, we are not. The animals all belong to God, not to humans. And, surely, the world does not revolve around us.

Blessing of the Animals

We are gathered here in the midst of these _____
(name the endangered species) today to remember that they
are also children of God. We have often destroyed you, taken
from you the places that you live, ruined your homes, and
done so thoughtlessly. Today we promise that we will do
everything in our power to restore your place on this planet.
We ask for God's blessing on all of you, and we ask for your
forgiveness. We will strive to live with you in peace from this
day forward. Amen.

Memorial Services for Pets

In general, memorial services for pets can be conducted at a
site where the pet is buried or at another location with the
pet's ashes present. As with any worship or ritual event, careful consideration needs to be given to whom will be in atten-
dance, especially with children; who will conduct the liturgy;
and what the focus will be. You might be surprised to know
that there are good resources already available. The Uniting
Church in Australia in its publication *Uniting in Worship*
includes two prayers for use at the death of a pet. This is one
of them:

> Loving God, you created us and all living beings
> For beauty, for happiness, for one another.
> With all our hearts, WE THANK YOU, O GOD.
> For all life that comes from you;
> The growth in the garden,
> The pets who are our friends;
> The people whom we love;
> With all our hearts, WE THANK YOU, O GOD.
> For the delight we have known in _____ (name of pet/
> animal)

In times of play, through moments of anxiety;
In the companionship of passing years;
With all our hearts, WE THANK YOU, O GOD.
O God, smile on our hearts,
Saddened by the loss of this beloved pet
Who inspired in us a love for all your creation.
Praise to you, O God, for the gift of life
And for the love of _____ (name of pet/animal)
With all our hearts, WE THANK YOU, O GOD.[2]

Additional Resources

Christian Organizations Addressing Animal Issues

all-creatures.org

http://www.all-creatures.org/

I include this at the top of the list because it has links to so many other sources as well. It is a wealth of information. The site includes action alerts, animal stories, poetry, Bible studies, and more.

AnimalChaplains.com

http://www.animalchaplains.com/

This interfaith organization provides information about pet memorial services and pet blessings, and information about becoming an animal chaplain

AnimalFamilies.org

http://www.russellministries.org

This is a division of Russell Ministries, a nondenominational group working on various environmental issues.

Catholic Concern for Animals

http://www/all-creatures.org/cal/

This group publishes *The Ark*, a quarterly journal devoted to issues of Catholicism and animals.

Christian Vegetarian Association

http://www.all-creatures.org/cva/default.htm

This international, nondenominational organization provides support for Christians who have chosen a vegetarian life. It is an environmental, animal activist, and healthy lifestyle organization.

The Episcopal Network for Animal Welfare

http://www.franciscan-anglican.com/enaw/

The goal of this group is to create a mutually supportive organization for Episcopalians who are animal welfare advocates.

The Healing Species

http://www.healingspecies.org/index.htm

This organization, not directly affiliated with a Christian group, connects children and teenagers with homeless animals. A variety of programs that could be applied elsewhere are outlined on their site.

Vegetarian Friends

http://vegetarianfriends.nfshost.com/

Affiliated with the Society of Friends, or Quakers, Vegetarian Friends publishes a monthly journal, *The Peaceable Table*, and provides support for Quakers who are concerned with animal welfare.

Secular Organizations Addressing Issues of Animals in Christianity

These organizations all consider issues of animals in relationship to religious traditions. Many have good information in their online resource collections and provide contact information for more in-depth resource support.

Best Friends Animal Society, Kanab, Utah

Animals and Religion Network

http://network.bestfriends.org/groups/religion/default.aspx

As part of the networking portion of the Best Friends Society and Sanctuary, this site provides connections for people interested in the topic of animals and religion. Best Friends is one of the largest sancutaries in the U.S.

Humane Society of the United States, Washington, D.C.

Faith Outreach Program

http://Humanesociety.org/faith

This site includes statements from various faith groups, the faith outreach booklet series, press releases, and campaign ideas.

ReligionLink.com

http://www.religionlink.com/category/doctrine/
animals-doctrine-practice-2

This page contains a list of resources for religion and animals in various traditions.

Books and Articles

In addition to the Works Cited, the reader is directed to the following sources of information and ideas.

Adams, Carol. *Prayers for Animals*. New York: Continuum, 2004.
———— and Marjorie Procter-Smith. "Taking Life or 'Taking on Life'? Table Talk and Animals." In *Ecofeminism and the Sacred*, edited by Carol Adams. New York: Continuum, 1995.
Akers, Keith. *The Lost Religion of Jesus: Simple Living and Nonviolence in Early Christianity*. New York: Lantern Books, 2000.
Amory, Cleveland. *Man Kind? Our Incredible War on Wildlife*. New York: Harper & Row, 1974.
Bekoff, Marc. "Increasing Our Compassion Footprint: The Animals' Manifesto." *Zygon* 43, no. 4 (2008): 771–81.

Berry, Ryan. *Food for the Gods: Vegetarianism and the World's Religions.* New York: Pythagorean, 1998.

Brock, Rita Nakashima, and Rebecca Parker. *Saving Paradise: How Christianity Traded Love of This World for Crucifixion and Empire.* Boston: Beacon, 2008.

Cavalieri, Paola. *The Animal Question: Why Non-Human Animals Deserve Human Rights.* Translated by Catherine Woollard. New York: Oxford University Press, 2001.

Clark, Henry. *The Ethical Mysticism of Albert Schweitzer: A Study of the Sources and Significance of Schweitzer's Philosophy of Civilization.* Boston: Beacon, 1962.

Clark, Stephen. *The Moral Status of Animals.* New York: Oxford University Press, 1984.

Coetzee, J. M. *The Lives of Animals.* Princeton: Princeton University Press, 1999.

DeGrazia, David. *Animal Rights: A Very Short Introduction.* Oxford: Oxford University Press, 2002.

Donovan, Josephine. "Animal Rights and Feminist Theory." *Signs* 15 (1990): 350–75.

Kalof, Linda, and Amy Fitzgerald, eds. *The Animals Reader: The Essential Classic and Contemporary Writings.* New York: Berg, 2007.

Katz, John. *The New Work of Dogs: Tending to Life, Love, and Family.* New York: Villard, 2003.

Kistler, John. *People Promoting and People Opposing Animal Rights: In Their Own Words.* Westport: Greenwood Press, 2002.

Kowalski, Gary. *The Bible According to Noah: Theology as if Animals Mattered.* New York: Lantern Books, 2001.

———. *The Souls of Animals.* Walpole, N.H.: Stillpoint, 1991.

Kurz, Gary. *Cold Noses at the Pearly Gates: A Book of Hope for Those Who Have Lost a Pet.* New York: Citadel, 2008.

Laland, Stephanie. *Animal Angels.* Boston: Conari Press, 1998.

Linzey, Andrew. *Animal Theology.* Urbana: University of Illinois Press, 1995.

Masson, Jeffrey, and Susan McCarthy. *When Elephants Weep: The Emotional Lives of Animals.* New York: Delacorte, 1995.

Noddings, Nel. *Caring: A Feminist Approach to Ethics and Moral Education.* Berkeley: University of California Press, 1984.

Pelikan, Jaroslav. *Luther's Works Companion Volume: Luther the Expositor.* Saint Louis: Concordia Publishing House, 1959.

Pluhar, Evelyn. *Beyond Prejudice: The Moral Significance of Human and Nonhuman Animals*. Durham, N.C.: Duke University Press, 1995.

Randour, Mary Lou. *Animal Grace: Entering a Spiritual Relationship with Our Fellow Creatures*. Novato, Calif.: New World Library, 2000.

Regan, Tom, and Peter Singer, eds. *Animal Rights and Human Obligations*. Englewood Cliffs, N.J.: Prentice-Hall, 1989.

Spiegel, Marjorie. *The Dreaded Comparison: Human and Animal Slavery*. New York: Mirror Books, 1996.

Sunstein, Cass, and Martha Nussbaum, eds. *Animal Rights: Current Debates and New Directions*. Oxford: Oxford University Press, 2006.

Waldau, Paul, and Kimberly Patton, eds. *A Communion of Subjects: Animals in Religion, Science and Ethics*. New York: Columbia University Press, 2007.

Webb, Stephen. *Good Eating*. Grand Rapids: Brazos Press, 2001.

Wintz, Jack. *Will I See My Dog in Heaven: God's Saving Love for the Whole Family of Creation*. Brewster, Mass.: Paraclete, 2009.

Young, Richard Alan. *Is God a Vegetarian? Christianity, Vegetarianism, and Animal Rights*. Chicago: Open Court, 1999.

Notes

All Scripture quotations are from *The Green Bible*.

Preface

1 Catherine Clement, *The Newly Born Woman*, as quoted in Schussler Fiorenza, *In Memory of Her*, xiii.
2 Flaccus, "Gone to the Dogs."
3 This is certainly not the first such attempt. Starting in the 1980s a few scholars began considering the role of animals in Christianity. See, among many others, Jay McDaniel, *Of God and Pelicans*; Andrew Linzey, *Animal Gospel*; Stephen Webb, *On God and Dogs*; Hobgood-Oster, *Holy Dogs and Asses*.
4 Fiorenza, *In Memory of Her*, xviii.
5 Fiorenza, *In Memory of Her*, xlvi.
6 Fudge, *Renaissance Beasts*, 4.
7 Fudge, *Renaissance Beasts*, 11.
8 García-Rivera, *St. Martín de Porres*, 2.

Introduction

1 Carol Adams, *Prayers for Animals*, 43.
2 Jackie, Kimberly, J.T., Beverly, Mark, Max, John, Shawn, Ken, Lilly, Janie, and more volunteers than I can possibly list (Jimmy, Curt, Joanne, Barb, Sherry, Lana, Debbie, Dave, Shawn, Tracy, Chris, Victoria, Cherilyn, John, Peggy, Jen, Jennifer, and it goes on and on and on).
3 The story is also told in the Gospel of Mark.

4   Throughout the text I will use the designations "B.C.E." (before the Common Era) and "C.E." (Common Era) for dating purposes.

5   Kay Warren, "Puppies Aren't People," her.meneutics, April 22, 2009, http://blog.christianitytoday.com/women/2009/04/kay_warren_puppies_arent_peopl.html, last accessed March 16, 2010.

6   "Not One Sparrow," 19.

7   Hobgood-Oster, *Holy Dogs and Asses*. 15.

8   I want to attribute this question to a book title, *Good News for Animals*; the book was edited by McDaniel and Pinches.

Chapter 1

1   Monks of New Skete, *I & Dog*, 6.

2   For more information, see http://www.georgetowndogrescue.com/.

3   The wonderful, patient student did foster Jazz after that and did a wonderful job.

4   See Verrocchio, "Tobias and the Angel"; Rembrandt, "The Angel and Tobias"; Pollaiuolo, "Tobias and the Angel"; and many more.

5   Names of the student and her dog are used with the student's permission.

6   Several recent findings of wolves in transition to dogs, possibly, suggest that the timeline is closer to 30,000 years ago. See Germonpré et al., "Fossil Dogs," for information on the discovery of a skull resembling prehistoric dogs in Goyet cave in Belgium that dates to 31,700 years ago. Vilà, Savolainen, et al. in "Multiple and Ancient Origins," indicate dates of up to 100,000 years ago, though this theory is controversial. Coppinger and Coppinger, *Dogs*, suggest the date of 15,000 years before the present as the most likely for the appearance of "dogs" with humans.

7   Haraway, *Companion Species Manifesto*, 12.

8   Humans are not the only species to "domesticate" another species. Ants do so as well.

9   Morey, "Early Evolution of the Domestic Dog."

10   See Diamond, *Guns, Germs, and Steel*; and Diamond, "Evolution, Consequences," 702.

11   For more information, see Godden, *Butterfly Lions*.

12   *U.S. Pet Ownership and Demographics Sourcebook*, American Veterinary Medicine Association, 2007. http://www.avma.org/reference/marketstats/sourcebook.asp (accessed December 23, 2009).

13   Pickrell, "Oldest Known Pet Cat?"

14   Schimmel, "Introduction," 7.

15   See Engels, *Classical Cats*, 10. Even in Antarctica, cats live under human protection.

16   Schimmel, "Introduction," 9.

17   Kors and Peters, *Witchcraft in Europe*, 114–16. Interestingly, Pope

Gregory IX, who published *Vox in Rama* as a papal bulletin in 1232, is the same pope who canonized Francis of Assisi.

18 Engels, *Classical Cats*, 184–85.

19 Barstow, *Witchcraze*, 76.

20 Sax, "Magic of Animals," 319.

21 Some of the same images of the Last Supper that depict playful or adoring dogs include a cat sneaking around at the edges with a sinister look.

22 Lehr, "Those Who Kept Cats Survived"; also see Engels, *Classical Cats*. The black rat, native to South and Southeast Asia, is the dominant carrier of the flea that causes the bubonic plague. This rat came to Europe on ships and in grain caravans. Without cats to control the black rat population, the plague likely spread much more quickly.

23 *U.S. Pet Ownership and Demographics Sourcebook*, American Veterinary Medicine Association, 2007. http://www.avma.org/reference/marketstats/sourcebook.asp (accessed December 23, 2009).

24 See Ovid, *Amores* 2.6 as explicated in Cahoon, "The Parrot and the Poet," 27–35.

25 Hilton, *Legends*, 7–9.

26 Hilton, *Legends*, 46.

27 Mallet, "Tender Hearts of the Saints," 507.

28 See "The Life of St. Brigit the Virgin by Cogitosus" and "The Irish Life of St. Brigit" in Davies, *Celtic Spirituality*.

29 This exception might have been made because his father was the governor of Panama and still held an interest in Martin's success.

30 García-Rivera, *St. Martín de Porres* (1995), 93.

31 Farmer, *Butler's Lives of Saints*, 18–19.

32 García-Rivera, *US Catholic*, 48.

33 Roheim, *Fire in the Dragon*, 44–45.

34 Luther, vol. 54 (*Table Talk*), 38.

35 Luther, vol. 54 (*Table Talk*), 175.

36 Niebuhr, "Faith in Gods and in God," quoted in Holler, "Is There a Thou," 88.

37 Buber, *I and Thou*, 18.

38 Monks of New Skete, *I & Dog*, 5.

39 See Dewitt, "Behemoths and Batriachians."

40 Heyward, *Saving Jesus*, 65.

41 Fretheim, *God and World*, 19.

42 McFague, *Life Abundant*, 143–44; emphasis in original.

43 McConnell, *Love Is Never Having to Say Anything At All*, 130.

44 Bekoff, "Dog Trust," 20.

45 Beckoff, "Power of Pets," 21.

46 See the National Council on Pet Population, Study and Policy, http://www.petpopulation.org/.

47 Heyward, *Saving Jesus*, 56.

48   There are countless resources for gathering information on puppy mills. Some places to start are http://www.stoppuppymills.org/; Peters, "Puppy Mills Face Greater Scrutiny," *USA Today*, October 31, 2007; "Anti-Puppy Mill Tactic," *The New York Times*, July 19, 2009.

49   I am indebted to an article by Tucker, "Creating Liturgies," for this terminology.

Chapter 2

1   The Triple Crown is the most popular horse-racing series in the United States. It consists of the Kentucky Derby, Preakness Stakes, and Belmont Stakes.

2   From Moran, "Eight Belles." Interestingly, Paul Moran, a journalist who has covered thoroughbred racing for decades, wrote an article the week before the Derby criticizing the decision to enter Eight Belles in the race. In that article he claimed that, in his opinion, "Eight Belles will be permanently scarred by the experience" (see http://paulmoranattheraces.blogspot.com/2008/04/eight-belles-deserves-better.html, last accessed on July 10, 2009).

3   The Jockey Club, the breed registry for thoroughbred horses in the United States, commissioned a new Thoroughbred Safety Committee in May 2008 in response to these tragedies.

4   In 2009, as I finished writing this chapter, Rachel Alexandra won the Preakness Stakes. She was the first filly to win that difficult race in eighty-five years. She did not run in the Kentucky Derby (the first leg of the Triple Crown); rather, she ran in the Kentucky Oaks that weekend, the race for three-year-old fillies. She dominated the filly field, thus her owner entered her in the Preakness. But he chose not to run her in the Belmont, the final leg of the Triple Crown. Luckily for horse racing, and obviously for the horses who ran, no deaths occurred as a result of the 2009 Triple Crown races.

5   For the purposes of this study, I consider sport to include activities initiated by humans with a primary purpose of amusing the human spectators/participants and, specifically, those that include other-than-human animals as objects of this amusement, as opposed to sports that feature only human participants.

6   Hunting for sport, horse racing, and dogfighting are the specific "sports" addressed in this analysis, but they are not the exclusive ways that animals are used for entertainment. Cockfighting, bull running, rodeos, and circuses, along with other less prominent activities such as using animals in the film industry, all come under this umbrella. Certainly zoos and similar animal entertainment arenas, such as Sea World, could be part of this examination; but the particular, complicated issue of zoos in the twenty-first century in the midst of wildlife conservation, captive reproduction programs, and education crises is probably worthy of its own independent study.

7   Elliott, *Apocryphal New Testament*, 370.
8   Spittler, *Animals*, 172–76.
9   Elliott, *Apocryphal New Testament*, 370–71.
10 Wiedemann, *Emperors and Gladiators*, 60.
11 Kalof, *Cultural History*, 117.
12 Toynbee, *Animals in Roman Life*, 21–22.
13 Wiedemann, *Emperors and Gladiators*, 59.
14 Elliott, *Apocryphal New Testament*, 378–79.
15 Eusebius, *History of the Church*, 336.
16 Eusebius, *History of the Church*, 200.
17 Eusebius, *History of the Church*, 146.
18 Tertullian, "Passion of the Holy Martyrs," 700, 705.
19 This report is from Martial, *De spectaculis liber* 14 (12), 15 (13), 16 (14) as cited in Shelton, "Beastly Spectacles," 116–17.
20 Thompson, "Martyrdom of Polycarp," 28.
21 McMurray, "AP Finds 5,000 Race Horse Deaths."
22 Bekoff, *Encyclopedia*. 1136. In 2006 the U.S. Congress passed the American Horse Slaughter Prevention Act, effectively closing down all horse slaughter operations in the U.S. But in 2008 approximately 120,000 horses were exported to Mexico and Canada for slaughter, according to the U.S. Department of Agriculture.
23 Xenophon, *The Art of Horsemanship*.
24 Drape, "New York Lags."
25 "NTRA Safety and Integrity Alliance Pledge," http://www.ntra.com/content/safetyalliance.
26 Pickrell, "95% of Thoroughbreds."
27 Bekoff, *Encyclopedia*, 758–59.
28 Paulick, "Death of a Derby Winner."
29 Maske, "Falcons' Vick Indicted."
30 Gay, "26 People Charged" (accessed July 10, 2009).
31 In Wayne Pacelle, "Eight-State Dogfighting Raid Largest in U.S. History," http://hsus.typepad.com/wayne/2009/07/dogfighting-raid.html (accessed July 10, 2009).
32 Pit bull terriers are not actually a recognized breed. Rather, a combination of a variety of breeds results in a mixed group of dogs popularly called pit bulls. It is a confusing and somewhat random designation. The breeds that are usually combined to make these new lines of dogs who are sometimes used in fighting pits are American Staffordshire terriers, bull terriers, American bulldogs, Staffordshire terriers, and, occasionally, small Rottweilers or boxers.
33 http://www.pbreporter.com/Guide%20to%20fighting%20breeds.htm (accessed on June 15, 2009). While the magazine is no longer in publication, according to its website the site itself was updated as recently as July 1, 2009. As of March 2010 this website had been suspended.
34 Roth, *Man Who Talks to Dogs*, 60.

35   Evans, Gauthier, and Forsyth, "Dogfighting," 214.
36   Henry and Sanders, "Bullying and Animal Abuse," 122.
37   See Henry and Sanders, "Bullying and Animal Abuse"; Flynn, "Battered Women"; Gupta, "Functional Links."
38   Roth, *Man Who Talks to Dogs*, 63.
39   I changed the dog's name here, since even after she was adopted, her new person kept her name and I do not want her to be identified.
40   For news on the July 2009 raid, see HSUS, "Dogs Cared for after Largest Dogfighting Raid in U.S. History," http://www.hsus.org/acf/news/ ex-fighting_dogs_071509.html (last accessed on September 2, 2009).
41   Hagiographies, a particular literary genre, are stories of saints' lives recorded or told for the purpose of edification; in other words, they have a pedagogical purpose and are open to interpretation. They should not be read as a "biography" necessarily, though that does not diminish their significance. For a more thorough examination of the lives of saints in relationship to animals, see Hobgood-Oster, *Holy Dogs and Asses*.
42   Voragine, *Golden Legend*, 147–48.
43   The deer has a symbol-rich history in European Christianity. Psalm 42 compares the longing of the hart or deer for running water with the longing of the soul for God. Based on that text, the deer is sometimes interpreted as a symbol for the soul. Deer have also been a staple of medieval European diets, so they are often hunted in stories as well as in real life.
44   See Proctor, *Bathed in Blood*, and Hermann, *Hunting and the American Imagination*.
45   By careful or skilled hunting, I mean skilled hunting that does not injure the animal without killing him or her as quickly as possible.
46   For more information, see Outreach Outdoors, http://www.outreach outdoors.com (last accessed July 15, 2009).
47   Scully, *Dominion*, 71.
48   Christian Sportsmen's Fellowship, http://www.christiansportsman .com/ (last accessed July 15, 2009).
49   The prices cited were gathered from these central Texas exotic hunting ranches: Rio Bonito Ranch, just outside of San Antonio; Circle E Ranch, north of Houston; Clear Springs Ranch, in central Texas. Similar prices are common and similar species can be hunted at a variety of exotic game ranches in the southwestern United States.
50   Bernstein, *Without a Tear*, 7.
51   Bernstein, *Without a Tear*, 117.
52   Peerman, "Unsportsmanlike Conduct," 10.
53   More, *Utopia*, 108.
54   Daniel, "Early Modern Olympians," 260.
55   See Ritvo, *Animal Estate*, for a general social history of humans and animals in Victorian England.

56 For a complete history, see the classic work by Ritvo, *Animal Estate.*
57 A film biography of Wilberforce's life, entitled *Amazing Grace,* was released in 2007 and has a particular focus on his role in the anticruelty movement and the establishment of the SPCA.
58 *The Parliamentary History of England from the Earliest Period to the Year 1803* (London: T.C. Hansard, 1820), 845–46.
59 From the Royal Society for the Prevention of Cruelty to Animals Annual Report, 1835. Quoted in Li, "Union of Christianity," 274.
60 *The Evangelical Magazine and Missionary Chronicle,* vol. 12 (London: William Clowest & Sons, 1834), 541.
61 For more information, see "Faith Outreach," HSUS, http://www.hsus .org/religion/.

Chapter 3

1   Luther, "Sermons on the Sermon on the Mount."
2   In addition to those listed above, numerous scholars have researched and published information on the centrality of food to human culture. Some of the most prominent are: Margaret Mead, David Carrasco, Claude Lévi-Strauss, Colin Spencer, Mary Douglas, Caroline Walker Bynum, Mircea Eliade.
3   A bumper sticker from "Restoring Eden" website.
4   The literature on food in the Hebrew Bible is too extensive to list here. One place to begin reading is *The Earth Bible* series edited by Norman Habel.
5   Hobgood-Oster, "'For Out of That Well.'"
6   A few of the most helpful studies are Astell, *Eating Beauty*; Dix, *Shape of the Liturgy*; McGowan, *Ascetic Eucharists.*
7   Francis of Assisi, "Rule of the Friars Minor," 1209 or 1210. English translation can be found in Armstrong and Brady, *Francis and Clare.*
8   Clare was the cousin of Francis of Assisi who, with his encouragement, founded her own order.
9   Bynum, *Holy Feast,* 138.
10 Sack, *Whitebread Protestants,* 97.
11 Statistics on meat consumption per capita and projected trends are available from the USDA. Specific numbers are updated daily (e.g., how many cows or pigs were slaughtered on that day). This information is available at USDA, "Briefing Rooms," http://www.ers.usda.gov/ Briefing/Baseline/livestock.htm (last accessed on July 17, 2009).
12 Statistics are available and updated daily at USDA Agriculture Marketing Service, http://www.ams.usda.gov/AMSv1.0/.
13 USDA National Agricultural Statistics Service, "Poultry Slaughter 2008 Annual Summary," February 2009.
14 Centner, *Empty Pastures,* 23.
15 USEPA (United States Environmental Protection Agency) Fact Sheet, EPA-821-F-04-011, issued September 2004.

16 EPA, "Regulatory Definitions of Large CAFOs, Medium CAFOs, and Small CAFOs," http://www.epa.gov/npdes/pubs/sector_table.pdf (accessed August 15, 2009).
17 Centner, *Empty Pastures*, 31.
18 Mukhtar, *Manure Production*, 2.
19 For a copy of the report, go to http://www.ncifap.org/; this commission was developed by a partnership between the Pew Charitable Trusts and the Johns Hopkins School of Public Health.
20 See http://www.cdc.gov/nceh/ehs/Topics/CAFO.htm (accessed March 19, 2010).
21 Zoonotic diseases are those that can pass between animals and humans, sometimes through a vector. Swine flu is the most recent example of one of these diseases that has received widespread media coverage.
22 Wuethrich, "Chasing the Fickle Swine Flu."
23 Wing, Cole, and Grant, "Environmental Injustice," 229.
24 Wing, Cole, and Grant, "Environmental Injustice," 225.
25 Wing, Cole, and Grant, "Environmental Injustice," 230.
26 For more information on the environmental impacts, see the EPA's report entitled "Potential Environmental Impacts of Animal Feeding Operations," at http://www.epa.gov/agriculture/ag101/impacts.html.
27 Pew Commission on Industrial Farm Animal Production press release, http://www.ncifap.org/ (accessed March 19, 2010).
28 Scully, *Religious Case*, 12–13.
29 USDA Animal and Plant Health Inspection Service (APHIS) info sheet, Veterinary Services Centers for Epidemiology and Animal Health, October 2008. Publications are archived at http://www.aphis.usda .gov/.
30 Bernstein, *Without a Tear*, 94.
31 HSUS, "Rampant Animal Cruelty at California Slaughter Plant," http://www.hsus.org/farm/news/ournews/undercover_investigation .html (accessed August 15, 2009).
32 *Eating Mercifully* is distributed at no cost by the HSUS. For ordering information or to watch the video online, go to http://allcreatures .hsus.org/.
33 For more information, go to http://www.rooterville.org/.
34 Several helpful essays addressing compassion toward animals are included in the works cited. See Adams and Procter-Smith, Dewitt, Habel (various essays in the five-volume Earth Bible series), Hobgood-Oser, Linzey, and McDaniel and Pinches.
35 Dunkerley, *Beyond the Gospels*, 143–44.
36 See HSUS website, Animals and Religion program, "Thousands Take Pledge and Religious Leaders Sign On to Help Farm Animals," http://www.hsus.org/press_and_publications/press_releases/religious_ leaders_and_thousands_of_others_join_to_help_farm_animals_ 100208.html (last accessed August 16, 2009). For more information

on the program, as well as the "Faith Outreach" program of the HSUS, go to these two sites: http://www.hsus.org/animals_religion/animals -religion.html and http://www.humanesociety.org/about/departments/ faith/ (both sites last accessed March 21, 2010).

37 Masson, *Face on Your Plate*, 59–60.
38 Masson, *Face on Your Plate*, 61.

Chapter 4

1   This blessing opened "Minding Animals," a conference held in July 2009. It was excerpted from Bradley Trevor Greive's book, *Priceless*. The purpose of the gathering was to bring together scholars, activists, artists, and policy makers who address issues related to animals.
2   For a helpful overview of the topic of biodiversity and species extinction, see Chivian and Bernstein, *Sustaining Life*.
3   Pohl, *Making Room*, 35
4   Three recent studies provide fabulous overviews and interpretations of hospitality in the Christian tradition: Russell, *Just Hospitality*; Pohl, *Making Room*; and Oden, *And You Welcomed Me*.
5   Nouwen, *Reaching Out*, 66.
6   The same strangers who came to Abraham and Sarah then go to Sodom, where Lot offers them hospitality at the expense of his own daughters. This violent, layered, problematic story has a long history of interpretation.
7   This story continues and focuses on issues of equitable distribution. The stone was large enough that no one shepherd could roll it away. The water was shared with everyone; no single person could monopolize it.
8   For a more detailed summary, see Hobgood-Oster, "For Out of That Well the Flocks Were Watered." See Genesis 29 for the story of Jacob at the well.
9   For an interesting interpretation, see Walker-Jones, "Psalm 104."
10 For a fairly comprehensive list of explicit references to hospitality in the Hebrew Bible and references to various Greek influences, see Arterbury, "The Ancient Custom of Hospitality."
11 See Pohl, *Making Room*, and Oden, *And You Welcomed Me*; also Mott, "The Power of Giving and Receiving."
12 Arterbury, *Entertaining Angels*.
13 For more information on this idea, see Crossan, *Birth of Christianity*.
14 Crossan, *Jesus*, 73.
15 A few examples from the New Testament are Acts 16:14-15, 18:1-3; Romans 12:13, 15:7; Hebrews 13:2; 1 Peter 4:9.
16 See Oden, *And You Welcomed Me*, for an in-depth study of early Christian texts and hospitality.
17 Quoted in Oden, *And You Welcomed Me*, 56.
18 Quoted in Oden, *And You Welcomed Me*, 64.

19 Jerome, "Apology in Answer to Rufinus," quoted in Oden, *And You Welcomed Me*, 69.
20 *The Golden Legend* was the most printed book in Europe from 1470 to 1530.
21 Voragine, *Golden Legend*, 213.
22 For an account of this story, see Ward, *Harlots of the Desert*.
23 See Ward, trans., *The Sayings of the Desert Fathers*.
24 Doran, *Lives of Simeon Stylites*.
25 See chap. 4, "Counted Among the Saints," in Hobgood-Oster, *Holy Dogs and Asses*.
26 From the "Dialogues of Sulpicius Severus," also quoted in Oden, *And You Welcomed Me*, 70–72.
27 Davies, *Celtic Spirituality*, 129.
28 Davies, *Celtic Spirituality*, 141–42.
29 This icon is currently kept at the Museo Sacro Cristano, Vatican City, Rome.
30 Elliott, *Apocryphal New Testament*, 94.
31 Elliott, *Apocryphal New Testament*, 95.
32 Davies, *Celtic Spirituality*, 163.
33 Davies, *Celtic Spirituality*, 187.
34 Dostoevsky, *Brothers Karamazov*, 319.
35 Carson, *Silent Spring*.
36 See Goodwin, *Rachel Carson's Silent Spring*.
37 For more information on toxic chemicals released where you live, go to EPA, "Toxics Release Inventory Program," http://www.epa.gov/TRI/.
38 For a very clear account of this process, see Mackay, *Atlas of Endangered Species*. Quotation from p. 15.
39 Mackay, *Atlas of Endangered Species*, 64–65.
40 The particular whales that Siebert was reporting on were "beaked" whales. They have a beak like a dolphin, and there are about twenty known species. These whales are among the deepest diving of all whales, which makes the occurrence of the "bends" in them even more startling.
41 Siebert, "Watching Whales Watching Us."
42 Malakoff, "Roaring Debate."
43 Chivian and Bernstein, *Sustaining Life*.
44 Statistics are available in various sources including Mackay, *Atlas of Endangered Species*; and Chivian and Bernstein, *Sustaining Life*.
45 Finn, Tregenza, and Norman, "Defensive Tool Use." This story was reported in a variety of popular news media sources as well.
46 Assateague is part of a United Nations Educational, Scientific, and Cultural Organization (UNESCO)-designated World Biosphere Reserve (the Virginia Coast Reserve). There are over 320 species of birds who inhabit the island along with numerous other coastal animals.

47 For a full study of the impact of domesticated animals on the Chesa-
    peake Bay region, see Anderson, *Creatures of Empire*.
48 Pohl, *Making Room*, x.
49 See Ricoeur, "The Golden Rule."
50 Kirk, "'Love Your Enemies.'" See also Topel, "Tarnished Golden
    Rule."
51 Russell, *Just Hospitality*, 114–15. This book was actually compiled by
    two of her colleagues after Russell's death.
52 For more information on the sanctuary, go to http://wolvesofsaint
    francis.org/ (quotation from LeFevre on website, accessed December
    16, 2009).

Chapter 5

1   From "A Religious Proclamation for Animal Compassion," launched
    by Best Friends Network. For more information go to: http://network
    .bestfriends.org/groups/religion/default.aspx (last accessed March 21,
    2010).
2   White, "Historical Roots," 1205.
3   For a clear explanation of various positions, see Santmire, *Travail of
    Nature*.
4   The first is the proclamation made by Martin Luther, at the Diet of
    Worms in 1521, as quoted in Dillenberger, xxiii. The second is from
    Bekoff, *Strolling with Our Kin*, 41.
5   Pelikan, *Luther's Works*, 50.
6   Steiner, "Descartes, Christianity," 119.
7   Barth, quoted in McGrath, 354.
8   Barth, quoted in Lewis, 207.
9   After the fall of the temple in Jerusalem during the Jewish uprising
    from 67 to 70 C.E., sacrifices were no longer a part of traditional Jew-
    ish religious practice. But during the lifetime of Jesus, this would still
    have been part of his religious experience.
10 This line is from a well-known hymn, "Are You Washed in the Blood,"
    words and music by Elisha Hoffman, Cleveland, Ohio, 1878. It is
    included in many Protestant hymnals.
11 From the hymn "What Wondrous Love Is This," words and music
    cited as "Appalachian Folk Hymn," in *Chalice Hymnal*, 200.
12 The popular children's hymn, "Jesus Loves Me," has a number of
    authors. The music was written by William B. Bradbury in 1862 (see
    Chalice Hymnal, 113). Anna Warner is usually credited with writing
    most of the lyrics, though additional lyrics are appended to the song
    in different hymnals
13 Kant, "Duties toward Animals and Spirits," 240–41.
14 From Origen, *Against Celsus*. Quoted in Santmire, *Travail of Nature*,
    50.

15 From Augustine, *De civitate Dei* 1.20. Quoted in Yamamoto, 80.
16 From Aquinas, *Summa Theologica*, as quoted in Linzey and Regan, 125.
17 See Yamamoto for an expansion of this argument.
18 For an interesting analysis of this trajectory, see Steiner, "Descartes, Christianity."
19 Descartes, "Letter to More," February 5, 1649; in Kalof, *Cultural History*, 61.
20 The Great Chain of Being is a long-standing hierarchical cosmology, probably dating from the ideas of the ancient Greek philosopher Plato. Generally, it places inanimate objects (such as rocks) at the bottom and scales up through lower forms of animal life, finally to humans and the spirits or divine beings.
21 Berger, "Why Look at Animals," 1–2.
22 See the following books by Ryder: *Animal Revolution*, *Animal Rights*, *Victims of Science*.
23 Though this is a much, much more complicated story. Increasingly evidence suggests that the decimation of the buffalo was directly tied to the decimation of the Native American people. Wiping out one species also wiped out the other culture.
24 Kaplan, "'Bizarre' Octopuses."
25 Leake, "Scientists."
26 See the work of Bekoff for his ideas about "wild justice."
27 Luther, "Sermons on the Sermon on the Mount," from *Luther's Works*, vol. 21, 320.
28 USDA, "Animal Care Annual Report of Activities, Fiscal Year 2007," http://www.aphis.usda.gov/publications/animal_welfare/content/printable_version/2007_AC_Report.pdf (last accessed on January 18, 2010).
29 See Bekoff, *Strolling with Our Kin*, chaps. 12 and 13.
30 Michale E. Keeling Center for Comparative Medicine and Research.
31 Laura Hobgood-Oster, Research Journal, May 2009. This is an unpublished journal that I keep for field notes when doing research. This quotation is from notes that I took when visiting the Keeling Center (mentioned above) in May 2009.
32 This poem, "To a Dog," was written by Branch (1875–1937) and is quoted in a number of books and articles about human relationships to dogs. It was probably first published in the *Saturday Review* in December 1928. For one publication of it see Laland, 19.
33 Schweitzer, *Out of My Life and Thought*, 240.
34 McFague, *The Body of God*.
35 While there are many positive things about blessings of animals, there are also aspects that can be problematic. For an analysis of this, see "Animals Return to the Sanctuary" in Hobgood-Oster, *Holy Dogs and Asses*.

How to Help: Ideas for Communities and Congregations

1   When I put this together, it was not intended for publication, so I did not indicate which words were my own and which were borrowed from the many blessings I have attended. If there are words here that I borrowed from someone and you read this and notice they are yours, please let me know so I can attribute them to you directly. It is my intention to directly attribute any sources I use.

2   From *Uniting in Worship*, 2. Also quoted in Tucker, "Creating Liturgies."

Works Cited

A Religious Proclamation for Animal Compassion. Launched by Best Friends Network. Text can be found online at a number of sites including http://www.peace4paws.com/proclamation.pdf.

Anderson, Virginia DeJohn. *Creatures of Empire: How Domestic Animals Transformed Early America.* New York: Oxford University Press, 2004.

Armstrong, Regis, and Ignatius Brady, trans. and Introduction. *Francis and Clare: The Complete Works.* New York: Paulist Press, 1982.

Arterbury, Andrew. "The Ancient Custom of Hospitality, the Greek Novels, and Acts 10:1–11:18." *Perspectives in Religious Studies* 29 (2002): 53–72.

———. *Entertaining Angels: Early Christian Hospitality in Its Mediterranean Setting.* Sheffield, England: Sheffield Phoenix Press, 2005.

Astell, Ann. *Eating Beauty: The Eucharist and the Spiritual Arts of the Middle Ages.* Ithaca: Cornell University Press, 2006.

Baraka: A World Beyond Words. Director, Ron Fricke. Mark Magidson Films. MPI Home Video, 1999.

Barstow, Anne. *Witchcraze: A New History of the European Witch Hunts.* New York: HarperOne, 1995.

Bekoff, Marc, ed. *Encyclopedia of Human-Animal Relationships.* Westport, Conn.: Greenwood Press, 2007.

Bekoff, Marc. "Dog Trust: Lessons from Our Companions." *Encounter* 22, no. 2 (2009): 20–21.

———. *Strolling with Our Kin.* New York: Lantern Books, 2000.

Berger, John. "Why Look at Animals." In *About Looking*. New York: Pantheon Books, 1980.

Bernstein, Mark. *Without a Tear: Our Tragic Relationship with Animals*. Urbana: University of Illinois Press, 2004.

Buber, Martin. *I and Thou*. New York: Scribner, 1970.

Bynum, Caroline Walker. *Holy Feast and Holy Fast: The Religious Significance of Food to Medieval Women*. Berkeley: University of California Press, 1987.

Cahoon, Leslie. "The Parrot and the Poet." *Classical Journal* 80, no. 1 (1984): 27-35.

Carson, Rachel. *Silent Spring*. Boston: Houghton Mifflin, 1962.

Cathcart, Rebecca. "Humane Society Traces Expensive Pups to Pet Mills." *The New York Times*, December 12, 2007.

Centner, Terence. *Empty Pastures: Confined Animals and the Transformation of the Rural Landscape*. Urbana: University of Illinois Press, 2004.

Chalice Hymnal. St. Louis: Chalice Press, 1995.

Chivian, Eric, and Aaron Bernstein. *Sustaining Life: How Human Health Depends on Biodiversity*. New York: Oxford University Press, 2008.

Coppinger, Raymond, and Lorna Coppinger. *Dogs: A Startling New Understanding of Canine Origin, Behavior and Evolution*. New York: Scribner, 2001.

Crossan, John Dominic. *The Birth of Christianity*. San Francisco: Harper, 1998.

————. *Jesus: A Revolutionary Biography*. San Francisco: Harper, 1994.

Daniel, Bruce. "Early Modern Olympians: Puritan Sportsmen in Seventh-Century England and America." *Canadian Journal of History* 43, no. 2 (2008): 253–63.

Davies, Oliver. *Celtic Spirituality*. New York: Paulist Press, 1999.

Dewitt, Calvin. "Behemoth and Batriachans in the Eye of God: Responsibility to Other Kinds in Biblical Perspective." In *Christianity and Ecology*, edited by Dieter Hessel and Rosemary Radford Ruether, 291–316. Cambridge: Harvard University Press, 2000.

Diamond, Jared. "Evolution, Consequences and Future of Plant and Animal Domestication." *Nature* 418 (2002): 700–707.

————. *Guns, Germs, and Steel: The Fates of Human Societies*. New York: Norton, 1999.

Dillenberger, John, ed. *Martin Luther: Selections from His Writings*. Garden City, N.Y.: Doubleday, 1961.

Dix, Gregory. *The Shape of the Liturgy*. New York: Seabury, 1982.

Dodson, Jualynne E., and Cheryl Townsend Gilkes. "There's Nothing Like Church Food": Food and the U.S. Afro-Christian Tradition: Re-Membering Community and Feeding the Embodied S/spirit(s)," *Journal of the American Academy of Religion* 63, no. 3 (1995): 519–38.

Doran, Robert, ed. *The Lives of Simeon Stylites*. Collegeville, Minn.: Cistercian Publications, 1989.

Dostoevsky, Fyodor. *The Brothers Karamazov*. Translated by Richard Pevear and Larissa Volokhonsky. New York: Farrar, Straus, & Giroux, 1990.

Drape, Joe. "New York Lags in Exams of Dead Horses." *The New York Times*, June 4, 2009. http://www.nytimes.com/2009/06/05/sports/05racing.html?_r=1 (accessed June 10, 2009).

Dunkerley, Roderic. *Beyond the Gospels*. London: Pelican, 1957.

Elliott, J. K., ed. *The Apocryphal New Testament*. Oxford: Oxford University Press, 1993.

Engels, Donald. *Classical Cats: The Rise and Fall of the Sacred Cat*. London: Routledge, 1999.

Eusebius. *The History of the Church from Christ to Constantine*. Translated by G. A. Williamson. New York: Penguin, 1984.

Evans, Rhonda, DeAnn K. Gauthier, and Craig Forsyth. "Dogfighting: Symbolic Expression and Validation of Masculinity." *Sex Roles* 39 (1998): 825–38.

Farmer, David Hugh, ed. *Butler's Lives of the Saints*. 12 vols. Kent: Burns & Oates, 1995.

Finn, Julian K., Tom Tregenza, and Mark D. Norman. "Defensive Tool Use in a Coconut-Carrying Octopus." *Current Biology* 19, no. 23 (2009): R1069–70.

Flaccus, Gillian. "Gone to the Dogs: LA Church Starts Pet Service." Associated Press, November 4, 2009.

Flynn, Clifton. "Battered Women and Their Animal Companions: Symbolic Interaction between Human and Nonhuman Animals." *Society and Animals* 8, no. 2 (2000): 99–127.

Fretheim, Terence E. *God and World in the Old Testament: A Relational Theology of Creation*. Nashville: Abingdon Press, 2005.

Fudge, Erica, ed. *Renaissance Beasts: Of Animals, Humans, and Other Wonderful Creatures*. Urbana: University of Illinois Press, 2004.

García-Rivera, Alex. "Come Together." *U.S. Catholic*, February 2008, 47–49.

———. *St. Martín de Porres: The "Little Stories" and the Semiotics of Culture*. Maryknoll, N.Y.: Orbis, 1995.

Gay, Malcolm. "26 People Charged in Dogfighting Crackdown." *The New York Times*, July 8, 2009.

Germonpré, Mietje, Mikhail V. Sablin, Rhiannon E. Stevens, Robert E. M. Hedges, Michael Hofreiter, Mathias Stiller, and Viviane R. Després. "Fossil Dogs and Wolves from Palaeolithic Sites in Belgium, the Ukraine and Russia: Osteometry, Ancient DNA and Stable Isotopes." *Journal of Archaeological Science* **36, no. 2 (2009):** 473–90.

Godden, Rumer. *The Butterfly Lions: The Story of the Pekingese in History, Legend and Art.* New York: Viking, 1978.

Goodwin, Neil, writer and producer. *Rachel Carson's Silent Spring.* A Peace River Films production for The American Experience. Cambridge, Mass., WGBH Educational Foundation, WNET/Thirteen, and Peace River Films, originally broadcast on public television in 1993.

The Green Bible: New Revised Standard Version. San Francisco: HarperOne, 2008.

Greive, Andrew Trevor. *Priceless: The Vanishing Beauty of a Fragile Planet.* Riverside, N.J.: Andrews McMeel Publishing, 2003.

Gupta, Maya. "Functional Links Between Intimate Partner Violence and Animal Abuse: Personality Features and Representations of Aggression." *Society and Animals* 16, no. 3 (2008): 223–42.

Habel, Norman, ed. *The Earth Bible.* 5 vols. New York: Sheffield Academic Press, 2000–2002.

Haraway, Donna J. *The Companion Species Manifesto.* Chicago: Prickly Paradigm Press, 2003.

Henry, Bill, and Cheryl Sanders. "Bullying and Animal Abuse: Is There a Connection?" *Society and Animals* 15, no. 2 (2007): 107–26.

Herman, Daniel. *Hunting and American Imagination.* Washington: Smithsonian Institution Press, 2001.

Heyward, Carter. *Saving Jesus from Those Who Are Right: Rethinking What It Means to be Christian.* Minneapolis: Fortress, 1999.

Hilton, Agnes Aubrey. *Legends of Saints and Birds.* London: Wells Gardner, Darton, 1908.

Hobgood-Oster, Laura. "'For Out of that Well the Flocks were Watered': Stories of Wells in Genesis." In *The Earth Story in Genesis*, edited by Norman Habel and Shirley Wurst. New York: Sheffield Academic Press, 2001.

———. *Holy Dogs and Asses: Animals in the Christian Tradition.* Urbana: University of Illinois Press, 2008.

Holler, Linda. "Is There a Thou 'Within' Nature? A Feminist Dialogue with H. Richard Niebuhr." *Journal of Religious Ethics* 17, no. 1 (1989): 81–102.

"House of Commons Bill to Prevent Bull-Baiting, May 24, 1802." In *The Parliamentary History of England from the Earliest Period to the Year 1803.*

Kalof, Linda, ed. *A Cultural History of Animals in Antiquity.* Oxford: Berg, 2007.

Kant, Immanuel. "Duties toward Animals and Spirits." In *Lectures on Ethics*, translated by Louis Infield. New York: Harper, 1963 (original c. 1780).

Kaplan, Matt. "'Bizarre' Octopuses Carry Coconuts as Instant Shelters." *National Geographic News*, December 15, 2009.

Kingsolver, Barbara. *Animal, Vegetable, Miracle: A Year of Food Life.* New York: HarperCollins, 2007.

Kirk, Alan. "'Love Your Enemies,' the Golden Rule, and Ancient Reciprocity (Luke 6:27-35)." *Journal of Biblical Literature* 122, no. 4 (2003): 667–86.

Kors, Alan Charles and Edward Peters, eds. *Witchcraft in Europe 400–1700: A Documentary History.* Philadelphia: University of Pennsylvania Press, 2001.

Leake, Jonathan. "Scientists Say Dolphins Should Be Treated as 'Non-Human Persons.'" *The Sunday Times*, January 3, 2010. http://www.timesonline.co.uk/tol/news/science/article6973994.ece#cid=OTC-RSS&attr=797084 (accessed January 10, 2010).

Lewis, Alan. *Between Cross and Resurrection: A Theology of Holy Saturday.* Grand Rapids: Eerdmans, 2001.

Li, Chien-hui. "A Union of Christianity, Humanity, and Philanthropy: The Christian Tradition and the Prevention of Cruelty to Animals in Nineteenth-Century England." *Society and Animals* 8, no. 3 (2000): 265–85.

Linzey, Andrew. *Animal Gospel.* Louisville: Westminster John Knox. 2000.

———— and Tom Regan, eds. *Animals and Christianity: A Book of Readings.* New York: Crossroad, 1990.

Luther, Martin. *Luther's Works*, edited by Jaroslav Pelikan. 54 vols. American edition. Saint Louis: Concordia, 1963.

————. *Luther's Works.* Vol. 54: *Table Talk*, edited by Helmut Lehmann and Theodore Tappert. Philadelphia: Fortress, 1967.

Mackay, Richard. *The Atlas of Endangered Species.* Berkeley: University of California Press, 2009.

Malakoff, David. "A Roaring Debate Over Ocean Noise." *Science* 291 (January 26, 2001): 576–78.

Mallet, C. M. "The Tender Hearts of the Saints." *The Irish Monthly* 61 (1933): 507–9.

Maske, Mark. "Falcons' Vick Indicted in Dogfighting Case." *Washington Post*, July 18, 2007.

Masson, Jeffrey Moussaieff. *The Face on Your Plate: The Truth About Food*. New York: Norton, 2009.

McConnell, Patricia B. "Love Is Never Having to Say Anything at All." In *Dog Is My Co-Pilot: Great Writers on the World's Oldest Friendship*, from the editors of *Bark*. New York: Crown, 2003.

McDaniel, Jay, and Charles Pinches, eds. *Good News for Animals? Christian Approaches to Animal Well-Being*. Maryknoll, N.Y.: Orbis, 1993.

———. *Of God and Pelicans: A Theology of Reverence for Life*. Louisville: Westminster John Knox. 1989.

McFague, Sallie. *Life Abundant*. Minneapolis: Fortress, 2001.

———. *The Body of God: An Ecological Theology*. Minneapolis: Augsburg Fortress, 1993.

McGinlay, Hugh, ed. *Uniting in Worship: People's Book*. Melbourne: Uniting Church Press, 1988.

McGowan, Andrew. *Ascetic Eucharists: Food and Drink in Early Christian Ritual Meals*. Oxford: Clarendon, 1999.

McGrath, Alister E. *Christian Theology: An Introduction*. Oxford: Blackwell, 1994.

McMurray, Jeffrey. "AP Finds 5000 Race Horse Deaths Since '03." *HorsePoint.com.au*, June 2008. http://www.horsepoint.com.au/portal/tabID_3435/ArticleID_2946860/DesktopDefault.aspx (accessed June 23, 2009).

Merchant, Carolyn. *The Death of Nature: Women, Ecology and the Scientific Revolution*. New York: Harper & Row, 1983.

Monks of New Skete. *I & Dog*. New York: Yorkville Press, 2003.

Moran, Paul. "Eight Belles Gave Derby's Most Valiant Effort." *ESPN .com*, May 3, 2008.

More, Thomas. *Utopia*. New York: Penguin, 2003.

Morey, D. F. "The Early Evolution of the Domestic Dog." *American Scientist* 82 (1994): 336–47.

Mott, Stephen. "The Power of Giving and Receiving: Reciprocity in Hellenistic Benevolence." In *Current Issues in Biblical and Patristic Interpretation*, edited by Gerald F. Hawthorne, 60–72. Grand Rapids: Eerdmans, 1975.

Mukhtar, Saquib. *Manure Production and Characteristics*. College Station: Texas A&M University System, Cooperative Extension, August 23, 2007.

N. B. "On Cruelty to Magazines." *Evangelical Magazine and Missionary Chronicle* 12 (1834).

Niebuhr, H. Richard. "Faith in Gods and in God." In his *Radical Monotheism and Western Culture*, 114–26. New York: Harper, 1970.

"Not One Sparrow." Editorial. *Christianity Today*, July 2009.

Nouwen, Henri. *Reaching Out: The Three Movements of the Spiritual Life*. New York: Image Books, 1975.

Oden, Amy. *And You Welcomed Me: A Sourcebook on Hospitality in Early Christianity*. Nashville: Abingdon, 2001.

"Old Hands Help Aspiring Farmers Put Down Roots," *Austin American-Statesman*, August 16, 2009.

Paulick, Ray. "Death of a Derby Winner: Slaughterhouse Likely Fate for Ferdinand." *Blood-Horse*, July 25, 2003.

Peerman, Dean. "Unsportsmanlike Conduct." *Christian Century*, March 6, 2007, 10–11.

Pelikan, Jaroslav. *Luther's Works*. Companion Volume: *Luther the Expositor*. Saint Louis: Concordia, 1959.

Peters, Sharon. "Puppy Mills Face Greater Scrutiny," *USAToday*, October 31, 2007.

Pew Commission on Industrial Farm Animal Production http://www.pcifap.org/ (accessed July 17, 2009).

Pickrell, John. "95% of Thoroughbreds Linked to One Superstud." *New Scientist*, September 6, 2005. http://www.newscientist.com/article/dn7941 (accessed June 1, 2009).

———. "Oldest Known Pet Cat? 9,500-Year-Old Burial Found on Cyprus." *National Geographic News*, April 8, 2004.

Pohl, Christine. *Making Room: Recovering Hospitality as a Christian Tradition*. Grand Rapids: Eerdmans, 1999.

Pollan, Michael. *The Omnivore's Dilemma: A Natural History of Four Meals*. New York: Penguin, 2007.

Proctor, Nicolas. *Bathed in Blood: Hunting and Mastery in the Old South*. Charlottesville: University of Virginia Press, 2002.

Ricoeur, Paul. "The Golden Rule: Exegetical and Theological Perplexities." *New Testament Studies* 36 (1990): 392–97.

Ritvo, Harriet. *The Animal Estate: The English and Other Creatures in Victorian England*. Cambridge, Mass.: Harvard University Press, 1987.

Róheim, Géza. *Fire in the Dragon and Other Psychoanalytic Essays on Folklore*. Princeton: Princeton University Press, 1992.

Roth, Melinda. *The Man Who Talks to Dogs: The Story of America's Wild Street Dogs and Their Unlikely Savior*. New York: St. Martin's, 2002.

Russell, Letty. *Just Hospitality: God's Welcome in a World of Difference*. Louisville: Westminster John Knox, 2009.

Ryder, Richard. *Animal Revolution: Changing Attitudes Towards Speciesism*. New York: Oxford University Press, 2000.

———. *Victims of Science: The Use of Animals in Research*. London: Davis-Poynter, 1975.

——— and David Paterson, eds. *Animal Rights: A Symposium*, Fontwall, Australia: Centaur, 1979.

Sack, Daniel. *Whitebread Protestants: Food and Religion in American Culture*. New York: St. Martin's, 2000.

Santmire, H. Paul. *The Travail of Nature: The Ambiguous Ecological Promise of Christian Theology*. Philadelphia: Fortress, 1985.

Sax, Boria. "The Magic of Animals: English Witch Trials in the Perspective of Folklore." *Anthrozoos* 22, no. 4 (2009): 317–32.

Schimmel, Annemarie. "Introduction." In *Cats of Cairo: Egypt's Enduring Legacy*, by Lorraine Chittock. New York: Abbeville Press, 1999.

Schussler Fiorenza, Elisabeth. *In Memory of Her: A Feminist Theological Reconstruction of Christian Origins*. New York: Crossroad, 1983.

Schweitzer, Albert. *Out of My Life and Thought*. Baltimore: The Johns Hopkins University Press, 1998.

Scully, Matthew. *A Religious Case for Compassion for Animals*. Washington, D.C.: Humane Society of the United States, 2007.

———. *Dominion: The Power of Man, the Suffering of Animals, and the Call to Mercy*. New York: St. Martin's Press, 2002.

Shelton, Jo-Ann. "Beastly Spectacles in the Ancient Mediterranean World." In *A Cultural History of Animals in Antiquity*, edited by Linda Kalof, 97–126. Oxford: Berg, 2007.

Siebert, Charles. "Watching Whales Watching Us." *New York Magazine*, July 8, 2009.

Singer, Peter. *Animal Liberation*. New York: Random House, 1975.

Smith, Alisa and J. B. MacKinnon. *Plenty: One Man, One Woman, and a Raucous Year of Eating Locally*. New York: Harmony, 2007.

Spittler, Janet. *Animals in the Apocryphal Acts of the Apostles*. Tubingen: Mohr Siebeck, 2008.

Steiner, Gary. "Descartes, Christianity, and Contemporary Speciesism." In *A Communion of Subjects: Animals in Religion, Science, and Ethics*, edited by Paul Waldau and Kimberly Patton, 117–31. New York: Columbia University Press, 2007.

Tertullian, "The Passion of the Holy Martyrs Perpetua and Felicitas." In *The Ante-Nicene Fathers*, vol. 4, edited by Roberts and Donaldson. New York: Scribner's, 1926.

Thompson, Leonard. "The Martyrdom of Polycarp: Death in the Roman Games." *The Journal of Religion* 82, no. 1 (2002): 27–52.

Topel, John. "The Tarnished Golden Rule: The Inescapable Radicalness of Christian Ethics." *Theological Studies* 59 (1998): 475–85.

Toynbee, Jocelyn M. C. *Animals in Roman Life and Art*. Ithaca: Cornell University Press, 1973.

Tucker, Karen B. Westerfield. "Creating Liturgies 'In the Gaps.'" *Liturgy* 22, no. 3 (2007): 65–71.

Vilà, Carles, Peter Savolainen, Jesu E. Maldonado, Isabel Amorim, John Rice, Rodney Honeycutt, Keith Crandall, Joakim Lundeberg, Robert Wayne. "Multiple and Ancient Origins of the Domestic Dog." *Science* 276 (June 13, 1997): 1687–90.

Voragine, Jacobus. *The Golden Legend: Readings on the Saints*. Translated by William Granger Ryan. Princeton: Princeton University Press, 1993.

Walker-Jones, Arthur. "Psalm 104: A Celebration of Vanua." In *The Earth Story in the Psalms and the Prophets*. New York: Sheffield Academic Press, 2001.

Ward, Benedicta. *Harlots of the Desert: A Study of Repentance in Early Monastic Sources*. Collegeville, Minn.: Cistercian Publications, 1987.

———, translator. *The Sayings of the Desert Fathers*. Collegeville, Minn.: Cistercian Publications, 1987.

Webb, Stephen. *On God and Dogs: A Christian Theology of Compassion for Animals*. New York: Oxford University Press, 2002.

White, Lynn, Jr. "The Historical Roots of our Ecological Crisis." *Science* 155 (March 10, 1967): 1203–7.

Wiedemann, Thomas. *Emperors and Gladiators*. London: Routledge, 1995.

Wing, Steve, Dana Cole, and Gary Grant. "Environmental Injustice in North Carolina's Hog Industry." *Environmental Health Perspectives* 108, no. 3 (2000): 225–31.

Wuethrich, Bernice. "Chasing the Fickle Swine Flu." *Science* 299 (March 7, 2003): 1502–5.

Yamamoto, Dorothy. "Aquinas and Animals: Patrolling the Boundary?" In *Animals on the Agenda,* edited by Andrew Linzey and Dorothy Yamamoto, 80–89. Urbana: University of Illinois Press, 1998.

Xenophon. *The Art of Horsemanship.* In *Scripta Minora.* Cambridge: Harvard University Press, 1968.

Index